BOSS
LADIES
OF
CLE

boss (noun)
ˈbäs | ˈbȯs
// a person who exercises control or authority

lady (noun, often attributive)
la•dy | ˈlā-dē
// WOMAN, FEMALE —often used in a courteous reference

—Merriam-Webster

BOSS LADIES OF CLE

Stories from
20 women
in their own words

Maggie Sullivan
Design by Monica Farag

Written, photographed,
and designed in Cleveland

For all the women in
Cleveland with an idea

FIRST EDITION

Published by Media Lady Press

ISBN 978-1-5011-7321-9

CON
TEN
TS

9	*Introduction*
11	*Valerie Mayen* - Owner and founder of Yellowcake
21	*Margaret Bernstein* - Journalist, author, and literacy advocate
31	*Mary Verdi-Fletcher* - Founder and artistic director of Dancing Wheels
41	*Justice Melody J. Stewart* - Ohio Supreme Court
51	*Jill Vedaa* - Chef and co-owner of Salt+
51	*Jessica Parkison* - General manager and co-owner of Salt+
69	*Malaz Elgemiabby* - Interdisciplinary designer and founding principal of ELMALAZ
79	*Julia Kuo* - Illustrator
89	*Jodi Berg* - President and CEO of Vitamix
101	*Jasmin Santana* - Cleveland City Councilwoman, Ward 14
111	*Jackie Wachter* - Cofounder and creative director of FOUNT
121	*Ahlam Abbas* - CEO and founder of Dirty Lamb
133	*Sam Flowers* - Musician, entrepreneur, educator, and cultural advocate
133	*Brittany Benton* - Musician, entrepreneur, educator, and cultural advocate
151	*Kathy Blackman* - Founder and owner of Grog Shop and B-Side Lounge
159	*Stephanie Sheldon* - Founder and creative CEO of Cleveland Flea, life and business coach
169	*Jasmyn Carter* - Entertainer
177	*Anjua Maximo* - Co-owner of GrooveRyde
187	*Erin Huber Rosen* - Founder and executive director of Drink Local, Drink Tap
197	*Heidi Cressman* - Engineer and director of diversity and inclusion at The University of Akron

BOSS
LADY
MANIFESTO

Create a vision.
Start now. What do you have to lose?
Sometimes the path you're on is going the wrong way.
You're never too old or too young to make a change.
You may not know exactly what you're doing, but you can learn.
Don't use location as an excuse not to get started.
Working in Cleveland offers advantages like affordability, community, a central location, and the chance to be renowned.
Linking your personal idea of success with helping others will help you exponentially.
There will be sacrifices—relationships, time, a steady paycheck, mental health, sleep, and more.
If you wait for perfection, it'll never happen.
The journey to Boss Ladydom is not going to be easy, fast, or glamorous. You will make mistakes and be misunderstood. Work, then work some more, and be persistent.

Introduction

Over the past year, I've had the joy and privilege of interviewing twenty women working in different industries who are making it right here in Cleveland. They're running businesses that have become the pulse of their neighborhoods. They're transforming local policy and striving to create more equitable communities. Their idealism is shifting conversations and laying the foundation for a sustainable future. They'll make you laugh and believe that anything is possible. They're leaders and innovators. They're the embodiment of Boss Ladies.

These twenty women are also graciously candid. Their stories would not be complete without revealing the staggering lows, ongoing challenges, and frustrating barriers they have faced—and continue to face—while pursuing the work they love. Many success stories fail to show that women have endured sleepless nights, sacrificed time with loved ones, struggled financially, experienced discrimination, and battled emotional hardships to build their careers. We are fortunate that these twenty incredible women courageously opened up about their experiences to help us make sense of and guide us through our own journeys.

To me, a Boss Lady is someone who boldly chooses her own direction, often asking, "Why not me? Why not be the first, the few, or even the only person to do what I'm doing? Why not take a risk? Why not dream big in pursuit of a better world?" And, for the purposes of this book, "Why not here, in Cleveland?"

This book was created with three primary goals in mind:

1. Allow the voices of diverse women to be heard and celebrated

In every interview, there seemed to be a few common themes: Cleveland is amazing but it's also a boy's club, it's segregated, and it can do a lot more to better serve its residents. While the voices of twenty women are a far cry from providing complete and unbiased representation of Cleveland's population, there is still much to learn and achieve by championing their perspectives. In the pages to follow, you'll hear from them about the grit it takes to be a Boss Lady, their unique challenges, and their visions for a better Cleveland.

2. Craft an authentic, attainable portrait of success and hardworking women in Cleveland

There seems to be a troubling, unspoken narrative that people from Cleveland need to move to another city to realize their dreams or achieve some canned version of success. But the reality is that anyone can do anything in Cleveland. These women prove that you don't need to move to L.A. to work in the music business, New York to be a fashion designer, or Washington, D.C., to make a difference.

3. Provide a real-life resource for local women to turn to for inspiration and advice

Each woman in this book is a reflection of what is possible. They offer practical advice to anyone looking to pursue a similar path and provide insight into what the peaks and valleys on that path might look like. Taken together, their stories paint a clear picture that you can accomplish whatever you're striving to achieve right here in Cleveland.

The photos of the women in this book are meant to be spontaneous, fun, and real. There was no advance location planning, no fancy camera, no studio lighting, and no makeup artists. The women were photographed wearing everyday clothes in their natural working environment, so that they all look like their authentic, beautiful selves. Most shots were captured on my Android phone. I believe this makes the project more genuine, and embodies the endearing, scrappy spirit of Cleveland.

I hope you're delighted by these stories. I hope it brings a smile to your face—like it did to mine—to learn that James Beard Award-nominated chef Jill Vedaa did not go to culinary school. I hope these stories radicalize you. I hope you're shocked to learn that Mary Verdi-Fletcher is still fighting for people with disabilities to have the opportunity to earn a degree in dance, or just enroll in a dance class. I hope you identify with these stories. I hope you can relate to the mothers grappling with the expectation to "do it all" or the women who have had to reinvent themselves over and over again. I hope you can find a perspective that's different from your own in these pages and learn from it.

More than anything, I hope you're inspired to go full steam ahead in building your own Boss Lady dreams, whether that's starting a business, running for office, making art, saving lives, raising a family, or something else. And I hope you realize you can do it here in Cleveland.

With gratitude,

VALERIE MAYEN

Owner and founder
of Yellowcake

From the cutthroat set of *Project Runway* to a studio of her own in Gordon Square, Valerie Mayen is using her corner of the world to make an impact on the fashion industry. As the owner and founder of Yellowcake, Valerie designs high-quality, functional clothing that's made in America and can serve as closet staples for years to come. This artist-turned-businesswoman is on a mission to provide sustainable, ethical wardrobe options while lifting her community up along the way.

Valerie in her Gordon Square studio

The beginning

When I was little, I didn't want to be anything in particular other than Rainbow Bright or Jem and the Holograms, which were '80s cartoons. In a realistic world, I thought maybe I would want to be a singer or artist.

My dad is a home builder, and he's also an immigrant. We were this very unconventional Latin American family living in a well-to-do neighborhood in Texas only because my father built us a house there and we could afford it as his business grew. But we still couldn't afford certain things that the other kids had. My parents would buy us clothes at thrift stores, or we'd shop at a store called Weiner's. All the girls I went to school with had the name-brand stuff of the time, so it was very obvious that my clothes were different. When I got into junior high, grunge was popular, and my mom started letting me do stuff to my clothes—I could rip, cut, sew, or paint on them in different ways. I got really good at taking my

crappy clothes and making them look more like me. Altering my
clothes really helped me gain confidence and do things I had
never done before, like audition for the choir and then become
choir president. It seems silly and frivolous, but fashion really helped
me do that.

I ultimately got my degree from the Cleveland Institute of Art in
illustration and graphic design. While doing a stint in L.A., I took a
fashion class at Otis College of Art and Design, which taught me
a lot about fashion illustration. After graduation, I was bartending
at a restaurant, and a woman I waited on took a chance on me
and asked me to make her a dress. I called up a friend who could
sew, and together we created a garment that we put a lot of
time into. The client took advantage of us—she didn't pay us and
took the dress anyway. After that moment, I decided to learn how
to do everything myself, including how to write a contract, price
garments properly, and ask for payment.

I took three classes at Virginia Marti College (now The North Coast College) on how to make a shirt, a skirt, and a dress. I couldn't afford to finish the program, so I bought a bunch of books and taught myself the rest, learning through necessity. My art degree wasn't really giving me the life I wanted—I was nannying, waiting tables, and working retail—so I figured why not try to pursue fashion? I practiced and practiced some more, then started putting a few dresses on Etsy.

The Manolo Blahnik of outerwear

At one point I read a book by Manolo Blahnik. His mentor told him to find one thing he loved and do it really well. He decided on shoes, and the rest is history. When I moved to Cleveland, I couldn't find a coat that was functional, looked good, and kept me warm. I also noticed that consumer trends indicated women can't justify spending a lot of money on something they only wear once. Outerwear is a utility product—it has more value—which justifies a higher price point. So I decided to make the best, most functional, stylish, appropriate, and versatile coat I could and become the Manolo Blahnik of outerwear. That's how we started gaining momentum.

I decided to make the best, most functional, stylish, appropriate, and versatile coat I could and become the Manolo Blahnik of outerwear.

I credit Project Runway for some opportunities in my life that I probably wouldn't have had otherwise. I had only been in business for a year and a half and had only been sewing for two years when I received an email from Project Runway's casting department encouraging me to apply for a spot. It was a crazy whirlwind when I was on (Season 8). After I went on the show, I did paid speaking engagements, which enabled me to grow the business a bit. Then several community development corporations emailed me about doing a pop-up shop to bring something fresh to their neighborhoods. We finally ended up in Gordon Square and had

YELLOWCAKE SHOP
ALL HANDMADE GOODS
ALL HANDMADE GOODS
YELLOWCAKESHOP.COM

YELLOWCAKE IS NOT GOING TO PROFIT AND BE SUCCESSFUL ON THE BACKS AND HEARTBREAK OF OTHER PEOPLE.

a storefront for almost five years. We hosted an annual fashion show, Hullabaloo, which benefited local nonprofit organizations and brought the community together for a creative, celebratory event. Eventually, Hullabaloo grew to such large proportions that I couldn't manage both the storefront and the event with a child, so we later scaled back.

Mission

For far too long, women and children have been marginalized and taken advantage of by the fashion industry. Yellowcake is not going to profit and be successful on the backs and heartbreak of other people. We're going to do it so the people we employ are also successful and well-paid.

We try to educate our clients organically about the negative side of fast fashion in a way that doesn't make them feel guilty. It's challenging because ignorance really is bliss, and the majority of what consumers see is the price tag. Even brands that claim to be sustainable are still employing women and children, marginalizing people groups, making T-shirts for pennies on the dollar, and selling them at alarming rates that are killing our planet and not really benefiting consumers.

To mitigate this, we offer garments you can wear year-round and that will last longer than most of the clothes in your closet. We provide personal customer service and custom modifications that happen right here in our shop. We create staple pieces that won't trend out. By making these promises to our clients, we're hopeful that those positives help them understand how to slowly change the direction of how fashion works. We just want to help people learn about what's going on, then let them make their own decisions about which businesses they support. We understand that you can't buy American handmade everything.

What is "success"?

From a business perspective, success means you're profitable and growing. From a lifestyle perspective, success is when you can support a cause and champion those without voices. The challenge is marrying the two.

I've sacrificed a lot of time and energy for this business. But those are the sacrifices we make now so that hopefully, in the next five years, we'll be able to delegate more, meaning I could take a break or an actual vacation. It's a lot like raising a child. Your business does become your baby—you raise it from the ground up.

From a business perspective, success means you're profitable and growing. From a lifestyle perspective, success is when you can support a cause and champion those without voices. The challenge is marrying the two.

I've gained a lot of fulfillment. It's rewarding to be able to give people a newfound confidence through clothing. We have a transgender client who has been with us since 2011, and she felt like we were one of the first female boutiques that she could walk into, feel accepted by, and know there was a place for her there. We've been there for clients before they were pregnant, while they were pregnant, and after they were pregnant. One of our clients got engaged in one of our coats and married in one of our dresses. And the people we hire become like family. Because we're succeeding, we can employ other seamstresses and help them succeed or even start their own businesses.

People might assume we have a lot of money because we run ourselves as a higher-end quality brand. They also might mistakenly think we're pricing our garments for the elite in an effort to get rich quick. But we're not either of those things—we price our garments so we can pay people. American labor is not cheap. I'm barely paying myself a salary right now; my staff gets a bigger salary than I do. People ask, "Why is this so expensive? Is it made of gold?" No, it's not made of gold, it's just made in America. People want American jobs, but they don't want to pay American job prices.

Best piece of advice

My advice for anyone interested in going down a similar path is to take your time and make a plan. Do all the boring and tedious things you don't want to do. If you put in the hard work now, growing and scaling your business will be a lot easier. Think about what problem you're solving. You don't have to reinvent the wheel, but you do have to find something that will serve people's needs. Also, offer your time and resources to your community or to other people in the business. Later, when you're in need, maybe you can call in some of those favors from the favor bank you built and people will be more inclined to consult with you. But you can't just go knock on people's doors asking for freebies.

Why Cleveland?

I choose to do this work in Cleveland for several reasons. It's a great city to start a business, raise a family, and live. It's extremely affordable. There are a lot of opportunities for artists here that people probably don't realize. It's where we built our following—we have a lot of loyal clients who live and work here and continue to support us, even if they move away.

Being based in Cleveland also keeps us central to the biggest markets that support our brand. Many of our clients are based in Chicago, D.C., Boston, Baltimore, or New York, which means we don't have to travel far to go to those regions for wholesale events and retail shows. I guess if we really wanted to, we could move everything to New York—but we'd have a fraction of the space at triple the cost. As much as I love being in New York, I also can't wait to get back home after most visits.

An ideal picture of Cleveland

It would be easier to commute between different neighborhoods, and there would be more diversity between neighborhoods.

MARGARET BERNSTEIN

Director of advocacy and community initiatives at WKYC, author, and literacy advocate

During Margaret Bernstein's twenty-four years as an award-winning journalist, editor, and columnist at *The Plain Dealer*, she uncovered stories that highlight the hope in communities that are too often misrepresented in the media. Now, she's the director of advocacy and community initiatives at WKYC. By building relationships with the people she reports on, mobilizing communities, and occasionally leveraging her superpower to put people on TV, Margaret has transcended the role of neutral observer and become an advocate for many causes, especially literacy.

Her efforts as a literacy advocate include expanding the presence of Little Free Libraries in Cleveland neighborhoods and promoting a culture of reading at home. She is the author of *The Bond: Three Young Men Learn to Forgive and Reconnect with Their Fathers* as well as two children's books, *All in a Dad's Day* and *Donuts with Dad*.

The beginning

All I really knew was that I wasn't good at math and I loved reading. I was the kid who would rather read a book than interact with other kids on the street. Looking at my natural talents, I knew journalism was probably going to be my best career path.

I was born and raised in L.A., which is a hard place to leave; you sort of think no place is as good as where you're from. It's a hard place to break into journalism because it's the number two market, so I applied to Gannett and other chains that were mining for talent and let them know I didn't mind going to a smaller market. Gannett hired me for a job in Huntington, West Virginia. I knew nothing about the city I was moving to. I don't think I was clear at the time that West Virginia was a separate state; I thought it was western Virginia until I did my homework. I spent three years in Huntington, working on deadlines and learning how to make my stories better every day. After that, I did what was really common in journalism, which is moving to a bigger paper every time you get a new job. I spent two years at a Tucson newspaper, then got a job as a reporter with *The Plain Dealer* and moved to Cleveland in 1989.

Advocacy journalism

When covering the minority community, it's very easy for any medium to fall into the routine of covering crimes and athletes. You have to go the extra mile to show that there are many other stories that just need to be uncovered. If you don't, you run the risk of just having criminal people of color on your news or in your paper. Poor news coverage of minorities is deadly because it creates a false sense that they're all like this. I'm just trying to show that despite the odds—and I want to show those odds—we have people making it.

There are probably two stories that most impacted my career, and one was covering the Imperial Avenue murders. There was a mass murderer, Anthony Sowell. People in his neighborhood had been complaining for a long time that they smelled things. There's actually a sausage store that was close to his home that got blamed for this smell. A woman went to the police and said Anthony Sowell had tried to rape her, so they went to his home and found the bodies of eleven women he had raped, murdered, and buried. They were all black. Deeply embedded in this story is the fact that eleven women went missing and it wasn't a huge uproar. The longest time one was gone was over two years. Families reported them missing, and nobody did anything.

By my count, four of the victims had received almost no coverage, and nobody knew very much about them. To honor all eleven lives lost, I got permission to write the life story of each one. It took forever to collect the information because the families didn't want to talk to the media. One woman said, "I turned on the news one day, and there was a dog missing on the news. I can't even get you to cover my damn daughter."

It took forever to build those families' trust. As I did, I looked for the hope. There wasn't a lot. Poverty had battered the families really badly. One of the sons of the victims basically had to raise himself. I was so drawn in by his story. His mother was thirteen when she had him. She was an addict, so they went from family member to family member until finally he entered the foster system, which was actually his saving grace because he got a good foster family. I've stayed in touch and learned that he just got his MBA *magna cum laude*, started a business, and named it after his mom. Keeping in touch with him sparked the realization that as a journalist, you have to do more than write about people. You have to look at where the failings were and see if you can help solve them. I stepped out of the neutral-observer stage of my career while covering the Imperial Avenue murders and became more of an activist.

> *As a journalist, you have to do more than write about people. You have to look at where the failings were and see if you can help solve them. I stepped out of the neutral-observer stage of my career while covering the Imperial Avenue murders and became more of an activist.*

Becoming a call-to-action columnist

Another story that greatly impacted my career started when I went to see the authors of *The Pact*, a *New York Times* best seller, speak while they were in town and I got a chance to interview them. *The Pact* is about three young black men who made a pact to stay

in school and become doctors. The book talks about how they struggle but they make it. I could have written a daily story for *The Plain Dealer*, but I saw something when I was at their speech that made me want to take more time and dive deep into the story. There was a busload of boys from Cleveland Public Schools who sat in the front rows completely enwrapped by everything these doctors said. I asked for more time to write the story because I heard a voice in my head say, "Go see if any of those boys made a pact."

I called their school and found out that they *had* made a promise to stick together. I wrote the story from their perspective—how great it was to meet the doctors, the similar struggles they were facing, and how the book was like their bible. One kid actually had *The Pact* next to his Bible. His mom had passed away the previous year, and he said those two books were the only things getting him through.

We also came up with the idea to ask readers to donate copies of *The Pact* for other kids in the Cleveland school system. We put that request on the front page of the paper along with the story and got a couple hundred donations of books. That inspired me to continue to do stories with calls-to-action. In my last two years at *The Plain Dealer*, I asked to be a Metro columnist. It took a lot of nerve on my part and definitely made me venture out of my comfort zone, but I knew I wanted to ask Cleveland to step up. The column, which ran twice a week, really became an exercise in what works and what doesn't in terms of lifting people out of poverty.

I sent the published article off to *The Pact* doctors because I wanted them to know the impact they were having. The doctors liked it so much, they asked me to write their second book. What would have happened if I hadn't done my best on that story?

What if I had just gone back to work, typed the article, and turned it in? You have to do your best at all times. You don't even know what the outcome could be. Because I followed my instincts, I got a book contract!

I took seven months off to write *The Bond*, which is about how the three doctors all grew up without fathers and the void they thought it left in their lives. Newly enlightened from the book leave, I came back to *The Plain Dealer* and wrote a front-page spread for the Sunday Father's Day paper about three Cleveland men who didn't grow up with fathers but taught themselves how to be fathers. There are so many societal reasons we have dads who don't know how to connect with their kids. I wanted to show that fatherlessness was a cycle, how hard it is to break, and that you need help. We had a very conservative editorial writer who wrote a column for the same paper titled "Absentee Dads, You Disgust Me." When I looked at the finished paper, I realized it would have simply had that column in it if I hadn't taken the time to go on this journey and show the different layers of fatherlessness. That one newspaper summed up what I felt I was able to bring to Cleveland through my work as a reporter.

Literacy crusade

I saw my first Little Free Library when I was at Miles Park School to do a story on the after-school program there. The students were excited about reading, telling each other, "I'm going to read this tonight, bring it back tomorrow, and get another one." I'd never seen anything like it at all. I knew I needed to find out who put it there and do a story on it.

After writing my first column on Little Free Library, readers sent in enough money to build fourteen more, and people wanted to know where to donate their books. From that response, I realized I was on to something. It was working on both sides—kids love it, and people want to support it. Somehow books soar over the barrier of racial tension; everybody wants a child to have a book in their hand. I wrote more columns about it. Every time I did, checks poured in and people would want to help.

Two years after that, *The Plain Dealer* announced it was going to lay off fifty people, and I was one of twenty-seven volunteers. I had already been getting very wound up about literacy. There are two things that any child who reads at grade level has in common, regardless of socioeconomic class: there are books in their home, and an adult is reading with them. All I want is for children who grow up in poverty to have that. I realized that a newspaper—a printed publication—is the worst place to be promoting literacy. The reason I left *The Plain Dealer* was to go on a literacy crusade that was not just about putting a book in a child's hands. I was determined to go totally grassroots and figure out how I could transform behavior in households to create a reading culture.

I planted at least twenty-five Little Free Libraries across Cleveland in my year off. Then I started writing storybooks for dads. I thought if I could write a book that a dad wants to read to a child or that a child begs their dad to read, I've created a reading-at-home moment that might strengthen the bond between that child and parent. One year after my layoff, I interviewed with Micki Byrnes at WKYC, and I told her, "If you love me, then you have to love my literacy crusade because there's no way I can stop now. In fact, if I can use the television platform to promote literacy, I am so in."

The reason I left The Plain Dealer was to go on a literacy crusade that was not just about putting a book in a child's hands. I was determined to go totally grassroots and figure out how I could transform behavior in households to create a reading culture.

My literacy projects in Cleveland have evolved to the point where they're very neighborhood-based. I want neighborhoods to feel pride in the fact that they wrap their arms around their children and put them first. The Little Free Library founder, Todd Ball, and I devised an idea that if a neighborhood pledged to put on one family literacy event per month, it could earn the title of Little Free Library Neighborhood. Slavic Village became the first Little Free Library Neighborhood in 2017. Then came Hough, Central, Collinwood, and now I really do have a vision of taking it across the city. I'm always exploiting the fact that people want to be on television—that's definitely the key to my success. I call it my superpower to throw at literacy: I can put people on television and they'll step up. When I started Slavic Village Reads, there was literally a line of other neighborhoods that were like, "We want to be on TV, too."

I used to put all my eggs in the mentoring basket. I was named National Big Sister of the Year in 2000, and my little sisters were both secretly pregnant when we got the award. One was twenty, and one was eighteen. I was acutely aware that as much as I poured into them, it was me versus the environment, and the environment won. I couldn't insulate them enough. At that point, I realized that just having a mentor is not the answer. But reading is definitely the great equalizer.

What is "success"?

Success means that in every neighborhood in Cleveland, there's an awareness that children need to read twenty minutes a day and that parents are part of that change. A child reading in Slavic Village is not because of me—it's because the neighborhood and the school both embrace the idea that reading is freedom.

Getting to the good part

I've sacrificed my weekends, my personal time...I'm blessed to have a husband and kids who understand that we're blessed, so we can make giving back the highest priority. Seeing people lifted up to a higher level just does it for me. I'm just getting to the good part. I honestly feel like I'm getting close to tumbling the snowball downhill. A lot of things are coming together, and a lot of people are deployed now in this literacy fight, so I just want to see what this looks like when it gets there.

An ideal picture of Cleveland

Young people are listened to, they're valued, they're challenged, they're actively mentored, and people of my generation understand that we have to do that. I think we have a lot of incredible building blocks in place, but there's a long way to go. I'd like to see Cleveland strengthening itself neighborhood by neighborhood, and I see the beginning seeds of that, too.

MARY VERDI-FLETCHER

Founder and artistic director of Dancing Wheels

Mary Verdi-Fletcher is the founder and artistic director of Dancing Wheels, a nonprofit integrated dance school and dance company that performs internationally. As one of the first professional wheelchair dancers in the United States, Mary has pioneered techniques that serve as a model for other art institutions. Her efforts as an activist have transformed lives and helped pass significant pieces of legislation, including the Americans with Disabilities Act.

Mary after a performance at Trinity Cathedral
Episcopal Church in downtown Cleveland

The beginning

When I was little I wanted to be a dancer—I always knew. My mother was a professional dancer and my father was a musician, so most of my bedtime stories were about her traveling throughout the country and how she met my father. It all sounded so romantic and fabulous, so I wanted to follow in her footsteps. But I was born with my disability, spina bifida, so there weren't even any dance classes for me back then, and it seemed like a pipe dream at the time.

I didn't know that society thought that I couldn't be a dancer, so I just kept saying, "I want to be a dancer." I used to walk with braces and crutches, and one of my braces would break all the time because I was doing little dances. Then I got a really strong brace, and it broke my leg instead—three times. After that, I started to use a wheelchair. It was a heavy medical model with armrests, which was a lot of metal to be lugging around. So, for many years I would just go to the ballet and watch dance competitions.

Changing legislation and lives

When I was young, I was hired by the first independent living center in Ohio as a personal care assistant coordinator. I developed training manuals that were used at the state level on how to care for someone living in their home on a daily basis, and I trained disabled people on how to be an employer to the person who was giving them care. We were advocating for independent lifestyles for thousands of Ohioans with disabilities.

The woman who led the independent living center was brilliant. She was a quadriplegic—paralyzed from the neck down. She would type on her computer using a mouth stick, and she wrote volumes that way. She was my idol. She took me under her wing because I think she felt I had the ability to speak out and wasn't afraid. We'd give testimonies at Senate hearings in Columbus and Washington since we knew legislation had to change. The laws at that time would give tons of money to nursing home facilities, but we had to find dollars at the national and state levels that could help people with disabilities pay a caregiver so they could live in their own home. Giving testimonies was part of my job at that time, but I also had the passion to see that some people of utmost intelligence were stuck in nursing homes because they had cerebral palsy and couldn't speak. Our efforts were a catalyst for statewide personal care assistance programs.

At the same time, mainline public transportation was not accessible. Cleveland had a door-to-door service, but that had a three-year waiting list, and it basically took you to the hospital or to doctor appointments. The Americans with Disabilities Act didn't exist back in the early '80s when I was an activist. There was legislation that instituted some accessibility, but it didn't give you the right to move about your community like everyone else. We became very militant. We learned how to take actions of civil disobedience from a national training group called ADAPT. We went to public hearing after public hearing. After making one last plea for the transit authority to institute a plan to make the buses accessible, we had no choice but to take action.

During the lunchtime rush hour, we rallied people to block bus traffic on a one-way street in Public Square. The people in wheelchairs went right in front of the bus and didn't move while our nondisabled partners got on the bus and told the driver to shut off the engine and allow their passengers to leave because the bus wasn't going anywhere. Then a second bus came, and we blocked that bus, too. The transit authority came out, and the media was everywhere. Back then, people with disabilities weren't doing outrageous things or challenging norms, for the most part.

After fifteen minutes or so, the police came and tried to drag us off to jail, except they were going to put us in the hospital instead because the jails weren't accessible. The paddy wagons were not accessible either, so they brought a door-to-door service bus to take us away. I said, "Oh, you can't take us to work or to school, but you can take us to jail?" And they drove that thing away so fast! It was incredible. After three hours, the transit authority made a deal with us to develop a plan to make every bus accessible. And they did.

Dancing through life

While watching local dance competitions, I kept on the sidelines at first, until a young guy came up to me and said, "Would you like to dance?" We started to experiment and saw that there was so much possibility in terms of partnering, especially in the ballroom style, so we started practicing together.

Once I saw the great possibility, I hung out at the local dance clubs. I was the only person in a wheelchair. I ran into my best friend from grade school, and her husband was a great dancer, so we started partnering together just for fun and eventually signed up for our first competition. I never told the competition organizers I was in a wheelchair—it didn't occur to me. I recognize my disability, but I don't lead with it. There were two thousand people in the audience of the dance competition, and we just busted out into our dance. For a smash ending, my partner came from across the floor and jumped up on my armrest and over my head. People went wild, we got a standing ovation, and we were chosen as alternate winners. That got covered by the media tremendously, and it spread like wildfire. People wanted to see more.

My partner and I started Dancing Wheels in 1980 and got performance requests all over the country. That year, I worked full-time at the independent living center and danced in seventy-two shows. For ten years, we were a for-profit dance company. Then I turned it nonprofit to do outreach and education, too. Cleveland Ballet bought the license, and I began to work with professionally trained ballet dancers, studied at the school of Cleveland Ballet, and learned a lot about translation movement and partnering. We established a school, and people with and without disabilities started taking classes together while we continued to tour at a more elevated level.

Still fighting

Building this company has its ups and downs. Dancers are transient, so I'm always trying to find dancers. Securing funding is highly competitive. We live in an economy that isn't always quick to support the arts—there are other pressing issues, like hunger and homelessness. I thought at this juncture that managing the day-to-day operations of the organization would get a little easier, but it hasn't. The more people you have, the more people you have to manage. I have employees and volunteers, but I'm still the driving force behind everything. When you're a founder, that's what you do. There's also huge joy. Seeing the awe on people's faces when we perform is why we do what we do.

Seeing the awe on people's faces when we perform is why we do what we do.

I'M PROUD THAT I'M SIXTY-FOUR YEARS OLD AND I CAN STILL DANCE...I ACTUALLY DANCED WITH NO KIDNEYS AT ONE POINT.

I think I have a pretty good balance of right and left brains. A lot of that comes from the fact that you have to navigate through problems every day when you have a disability. I work with some people who are linear thinkers. They work great as long as everything is working in a set way. But when there's a bump in the road, they're like, "What are we going to do?" I say, "Well, now we need to think differently."

It's stunning to me that so few people can go to a dance class in a wheelchair or with other disabilities. But being in a wheelchair seems to be the biggest separation for training. They can't get a degree in dance. I don't have a degree in dance. Teachers generally stay within the curriculum they're handed by the university, which doesn't include integrated dance. So we're still fighting. We're about to launch our certification program, which will enable integrated dance teachers to attain a level 1, 2, or 3 certification using our process and our terminology.

There's such a cry for diversity, inclusion, and equity, but people don't always think of disability in that—they think more of race and gender. I want people to see that it's equally important to consider people in the disability world. To date, the disabled community is still the most discriminated-against group in America. So that cry for equality needs to pervasive. I was at a conference for diversity and inclusion, and Senator Brown was giving a keynote speech in which he mentioned women, people of color, and gender differences, but he never once mentioned disability. He got off the podium and I sort of sideswiped him and said, "Excuse me, Senator Brown, I want you to know that the issues that relate to people with disabilities are so similar to all of these other groups that you're talking about, and you never once mentioned people with disabilities." Maybe two weeks later he was talking about inclusion on TV, and he did mention people with disabilities.

What is "success"?

If you set out to accomplish something, whatever that is, and you achieve it the way you envisioned it, then you're successful. I don't know if I'll ever achieve my own personal version of success, because I keep wanting more and dreaming bigger.

I'm proud that I'm sixty-four years old and I can still dance. I had one kidney removed right out of high school, then the second one went bad twenty-five years ago, and I needed a transplant. I actually danced with no kidneys at one point; I was on dialysis. My husband found that we were a match in three out of the six areas, so he donated his kidney, and a month later I was up dancing again. He saved my life.

Why Cleveland?

I never thought of living anywhere else and doing this. A lot of people in Cleveland are familiar with me and the work that I do. There's really good support here for us. It's my home. I've seen the progression of Cleveland over the years, and it's transformed beyond what I ever thought it could be.

You can't be afraid of work. You can't be afraid of speaking up. People will slam doors in your face—you can't be afraid of being declined or people turning you down.

Best piece of advice

If I knew what it would take to do what I'm doing, I probably would have hesitated to dive into it. I work 24/7. But then again, if it's your passion, your dream, your desire...you just need to know there's going to be a heck of a lot of work going on behind it. You can't be afraid of work. You can't be afraid of speaking up. People will slam doors in your face—you can't be afraid of being declined or people turning you down.

MELODY STEWART

Ohio Supreme
Court Justice

Melody Stewart believes in leaving things better than they were when she found them, including the justice system. After working for more than a decade in law academe and serving on Ohio's Eighth District Court of Appeals for twelve years, she made history in 2018 as the first African American woman to be elected to the Ohio Supreme Court.

The beginning

I don't have any recollection of wanting to be or do anything in particular when I was a kid. I just did whatever I was supposed to be doing at the time. I knew I would go to college, but I had no clue what I was going to be when I grew up. I'm actually still working on that, truth be told. The only thing I loved and had an interest in at the time was music—I played classical piano and classical guitar—so that's the only thing I wanted to study in college.

During my senior year at the Conservatory of Music at the University of Cincinnati, I got a ticket for going through a red light. I explained to the police officer that I didn't go through the red light—I was in the intersection when the traffic signal was orange and either had to complete the turn or back my car up. She gave me the ticket anyway. I was frustrated by it, so I decided to challenge the ticket. At the time, my older sister, who's a lawyer, was a prosecutor here in Cleveland, and she told me I didn't have a prayer of winning. I drew up a rudimentary diagram and presented it at my court hearing, and the judge found me not guilty. When I left the room, a couple of police officers came up to me and said, "Great job. I guess you're going to be a lawyer, huh?" I thought, *No, are you kidding me?* But that experience showed me that the justice system does work, so that probably was the first seed planted for where I am now. But I didn't think about law school after that, because I was just thrilled to be done with college when I graduated.

Do I really want to be a lawyer?

After college, I worked at a health-care management company and the vice president of the company had started law school. He would come in, set his books down, and go to his office to work, and I would peruse his casebooks. Corporations, property—everything I read seemed so interesting. I had worked for a year after college and was kind of intellectually bored. So I called my sister and said, "I'm thinking about law school. What do you think?" She was very quiet, then said, "I wouldn't do it if I were you." She said it was a lot of work, a lot of reading, and listed other reasons not to do it. I thanked her for her advice and I think I applied the next day—on a whim. The dean of admissions at Cleveland-Marshall College of Law offered me a fellowship if I attended full-time, based on my LSAT score and GPA. I still had undergraduate debt but ended up going full-time and working part-time. I think I spent all three years in law school and walked across the stage getting my degree thinking, *Do I really want to go to law school? Do I really want to be a lawyer?* But I knew the education and training I received would be invaluable, regardless of what I did with the degree.

> *I spent all three years in law school and walked across the stage getting my degree thinking, Do I really want to go to law school? Do I really want to be a lawyer?*

After law school, I got a job as an assistant law director for the City of Cleveland doing civil defense litigation. The law department gave me great hands-on experience immediately. Then I did similar work for the City of East Cleveland law department, briefly, because an assistant dean of student affairs position was created at Cleveland-Marshall School of Law, and I was encouraged to apply for it. After several years in that role, I accepted a visiting faculty position there and later at the University of Toledo. My mother had become ill with a neurological disorder, and I was her primary caregiver. The visiting faculty positions allowed me to have a more flexible schedule to care for her.

Making a run for it

Logically, I did not expect to win my first race for the Court of Appeals. I didn't know anything about running for office. It is a very political process, I was a political unknown, and I'm not a political person. I didn't have any political clout, and I didn't have any relatives who had ever been elected to office, so I had to create my own political presence.

One of my former judicial colleagues told me early on, "Politics is a game. You either play it or get it played on you." He was absolutely right. I had to learn that whole process in order to be supported and try to get endorsed; that took me two unsuccessful runs, which were in 2000 and 2002. I loved being in law academe, so it wasn't heartbreaking for me to lose either of those elections. Although I was politically a better candidate when I was elected in 2006, I think what really happened in that race was that no sitting judge who had more name recognition ran for the seat. The fact that no trial court judge ran in that Court of Appeals primary was luck.

While on the Court of Appeals, I was approached twice by the chair of the Ohio Democratic Party to run for the Ohio Supreme Court. But I wanted to do other things while on the appellate court and get a broader perspective of our judicial system first. After becoming more seasoned and gaining seniority on the Court of Appeals, I felt better suited to run. The third time I was approached, I agreed, but I knew absolutely nothing about running a statewide race. I raised less money than every other statewide candidate running for office that year. Because we didn't have a lot of money, I knew we'd have to be creative.

When I made the decision to run, I looked at it as an opportunity to crisscross the state, meet people, and educate them about why judicial elections are important. My primary goal was to reach as many people as possible in the state, inform them about the judicial system, and share my ideas for improving it. I tried to get to all the eighty-seven other counties, but I only reached sixty-two. Had I not won the election, my goal of informing people still would have been fulfilled. My running still would have been worth it. Now I get the opportunity to put into motion those things that I talked about on the campaign trail.

What is "success"?

Anything that helps a cause, an individual, or a community is success. Anything that I do individually or that we do as a court to make our legal profession, the judiciary, and the justice system better is success to me. The historical significance of being the first black woman elected to the Ohio Supreme Court is not lost on me at all. But if people can say, either while I'm on the Supreme Court or after I leave, that the judicial system got better during my tenure, then my work will have been successful. Being the first won't mean as much for me individually if I'm also the last for quite some time, or if it doesn't open the door for others to follow. Maybe my being elected will put in the minds of younger women of color that it's a realistic possibility for them now. I am humbled by, and appreciate this place in our state's history. But when I put on that robe, I know I've got a job to do just like my other six colleagues, and I have to work with them to get things done. We do things as a court. My being in the room can sometimes push the envelope and give a perspective that is different from theirs. I hope my service demonstrates that.

BE AWARE THAT THE PATH YOU'RE GOING DOWN NOW MIGHT NOT BE THE PATH THAT YOU'RE SUPPOSED TO GO DOWN.

Balancing act

Running for and being newly elected to the Ohio Supreme Court, I've sacrificed sleep—lots of it. Getting enough rest remains a challenge. I was the flavor of the month for Black History Month, Women's History Month, bar association events, law school commencements, various women's organizations, NAACP banquets...not that I'm complaining at all, but I keep thinking I'm going to cover enough of the state that people will tire of me soon. What I've gained is the opportunity to meet people I likely otherwise would not have had the chance to meet, as well as the opportunity to make a meaningful difference in our community and our justice system.

People may think that, as a justice, I make decisions based on my personal thoughts and feelings about things. I don't. I sometimes have to make judicial decisions that go against my personal beliefs and philosophies. It's not as hard as one would think, because even though I have to decide something based on what the law says, I still have the power of the pen in writing either a dissenting opinion or a concurring opinion, which is an opinion that agrees with the outcome of what my colleagues decided but for a different reason.

Even if it's something simple, do something to leave a place better off than it was when you got there. It shows that you're paying attention, you know what's going on, and you're invested in the operation.

I have the honor and privilege of being on the Supreme Court to conduct public service. It's more than just a job and a paycheck for me. If I were a practicing lawyer, I would do my best to help every individual client I had. As an elected official, I work on behalf of the collective.

Best piece of advice

My mother taught me when I was young to always leave a place better than it was when I got there. Every apartment I've ever lived in we've left cleaner than it was when we arrived. When I went to the Court of Appeals, I printed draft opinions doublesided. It saves the taxpayers a little bit of money, and it's environmentally conscious. Even if it's something that simple, do something to leave a place better off than it was when you got there. It shows that you're paying attention, you know what's going on, and you're invested in the operation.

For anyone interested in pursuing a similar path, I say go full steam ahead. But realize that you might not know what that path is or what it will look like right now. You may not see where it turns or where it takes you. Sometimes there are redirections—often seen as rejections—and they happen for a reason, even though the reason may be unknown to you at the time. Be aware that the path you're going down now might not be the path that you're supposed to go down. Stay open to being redirected.

An ideal picture of Cleveland

My nirvana would have clean streets; well-kept properties, be they public or private; world-class schools; a friendly, inviting atmosphere; thriving entertainment and business communities; low crime rates; no hate crimes; and frequent championship sports teams. Notice I'm not greedy—I didn't say championship teams all the time. Just *frequently*.

JILL VEDAA &

Chef, co-owner of Salt+

JESSICA PARKISON

General manager,
co-owner of Salt+

After spending years making their mark on Cleveland's restaurant scene, Jill Vedaa and Jessica Parkison teamed up to create Salt+, a Lakewood restaurant specializing in composed small plates, killer cocktails, and unique wines. Jill is a two-time James Beard Award–nominated chef, and Jessica is a leading general manager and sommelier. Together, they have popularized the concept of small plates in Cleveland while providing customers with a meaningful dining experience and gathering place.

The beginning

Jill:

I did not dream of being a chef. I was going to be an artist. I took every single art class I could possibly take when I was in high school, and that's what my focus was going to be at Cleveland State. Then I got a front of house job at a restaurant and kind of fell in love with it. I liked the pace, was getting paid really well, and only had to work three days a week. The people you meet working in the restaurant industry are characters—not only the people you work with, but also the people who walk through the door. It was fun to be around the energy of it. Eventually I worked my way into the kitchen because I wanted a steadier paycheck.

Jessica:

I knew I wanted to be a mom when I was a kid.

Jill:

She was highly successful [Jessica is a mother of six].

Jessica:

In high school, I wanted to be a chef. Then I had a baby and started working in the front of the house instead. I had an aunt who had taken me to Napa—she was a wine buyer for a major grocery store. I spent quite a while out there with her, fell in love with wine, and started my sommelier training. When I started getting into that, I was given more responsibility at the restaurant where I was working. I had been there for a really long time, and when one of my bosses got sick, they just kind of said, "Here are the keys," and I became a general manager.

Jill:

We met at a bar that Jess was bartending at. I came in with one of my best friends and ordered a bottle of wine, and we all chitchatted for a little bit. We became Facebook friends, and I never spoke to her again until three years later.

Do you want to open a restaurant?

Jessica:

After so many years, I got really tired of making a lot of money for somebody else. I came home one day and said, "I either need to get out of this business or open my own place."

I had gotten an offer to go into business with a woman who

wanted to open a wine bar, but it just wasn't something I wanted to do. Because my dad was a chef, I always knew that really good restaurants survive with really good chefs. I had seen on Facebook that the restaurant Jill was working at had closed, so I got in touch with our mutual friend and asked for Jill's phone number. Literally ten minutes later we were on the phone, and I said, "Hey, I don't know if you remember me or not, but do you want to open a restaurant?" And she goes, "Shouldn't we have lunch or something first?" And that was it. It took one lunch to come to the realization that this was something we could do.

> *I said, "Hey, I don't know if you remember me or not, but do you want to open a restaurant?" And she goes, "Shouldn't we have lunch or something first?"*

Jill:
When Rockefeller's closed, I didn't know what I was going to do because I had carte blanche there. I did all the menus, the wine list, beer list, cocktails, food, desserts—I did everything. I couldn't imagine not having that freedom. But I had never in my life wanted to open a restaurant. I thought it would be a pain in the ass. I had worked at a lot of restaurants and didn't want to be under the stress that I saw the owners were under.

But the only thing that made any sense to me was to open a restaurant. Jessica and I got along really well and had a very similar ideal of how we wanted the service, food, cocktail program, and wine program to be...

Jessica:
And aesthetically—how we wanted things to look inside and outside the restaurant. I said, "Let's just try to get a loan and see what happens." And we got one.

Jill:
I didn't have a lot of doubt. I knew that if we did something well, people would come back. It took some leaps because we had

RESTAURANTS ARE GATHERING PLACES AND SECOND HOMES TO A LOT OF PEOPLE. IF YOU DON'T WANT TO COOK, WE'RE HERE. IF YOU NEED A DRINK AFTER A LONG DAY, WE'RE HERE.

I'VE BEEN COOKING IN CLEVELAND FOR TWENTY-SIX YEARS. OUR SUCCESS DIDN'T JUST COME OUT OF THIN AIR.

never worked together, we didn't know each other, and she had never eaten my food before opening day. So there were personal leaps, but it really didn't stop me or give me a moment of "Don't do this."

Jessica:
We both were like, "What's the worst that could happen?" It fails. Okay. Is there a lot of money tied up in it? Sure. Time? Yes. Would your heart be broken? Of course. But life goes on. It's not rocket science. It's just food. It's just drinks. We're just trying to make people have a good time when they come out.

Challenges of cooking and serving in Cleveland

Jill:
One thing that we both always agreed on from day one is that the customer is not always right. That's not something that makes sense in this business. We had a very specific idea—an ethos of what we wanted this place to be. We don't do substitutions because what Jessica puts in a drink or what I put on a plate is there for a reason, whether it's texture or flavor. People want some sort of control over their experience. But we want to control their experience because we know how to do it better than they do. We've always had that mentality. There are no TVs in here, we don't give out free Wifi—we just want people to come in and enjoy each other's company and what's being put in front of them.

Jessica:
My biggest challenge—and she could care less about stuff like this—is reviews. Yelp and TripAdvisor. I've gotten a lot better with it.

Jill:
We'll do our damnedest to fix something, within reason. The people who don't say anything, then go home and sit behind a computer writing pages and pages of what they thought was wrong with this place—I don't care about those people because they're not giving us an opportunity to remedy whatever happened.

Jessica:
It's also such a boys' club in this business. Jill has been a James Beard Award nominee two years in a row. That's huge—it's like being nominated for an Oscar. There was press about it, but not a lot. We have, in my opinion, one of the best bar programs in Cleveland, and it never gets recognized. For small businesses in general, it's so hard to get your name out there without the

finances that back it. Advertising costs a lot of money, and if you can't spend $5,000 on a tiny ad, you can get overlooked.

Jill:
Every single city is a boys' club. I think there are a lot of young chefs in Cleveland who have literally zero idea how long either one of us has been in this business. I've been cooking in Cleveland for twenty-six years. Our success didn't just come out of thin air. We've been working very hard to build relationships with people and build our reputation as chefs and managers. Anything that stems from that is well-earned. I was nineteen when I started. When I got nominated the first time for the James Beard Award with Karen Small (owner of the Flying Fig), some people said we only got it because we're women. It was on the heels of the #MeToo movement. They would never say it to my face, but you hear it. I thought, *Maybe. Maybe they needed to recognize some women*...but I can't in recent years remember anybody else from Cleveland—male or female—who was nominated.

Then I got it again. It's awesome. If I continue to get nominated every single year and never even win, that's great. I don't go after stuff like that—it's not what drives me. I do this because I like doing it, I want to make good food, I want to serve something that people enjoy, create an experience, and keep pushing myself to make better and better food. If I get recognized on some level for that, awesome.

Losing sleep, gaining confidence

Jill:
I've sacrificed my liver. And sleep.

Jessica:
So much sleep.

Jill:
It's emotional.

Jessica:
It's very emotional. And I feel like you're not allowed to be emotional. You sacrifice a ton. Every single day, I sacrifice time with my family. Every. Single. Day. I've missed awards ceremonies, games, sleepovers. We've sacrificed relationships with people whom we had to let go because they looked at us as just being

Photo by Alyse Nelson

friends and not their bosses. It's a lot. We don't have the money to pay a general manager or an executive chef to be here 24/7; I'm the general manager, and Jill is the executive chef. I run the door, and she runs the kitchen on Friday and Saturday nights. That's really surprising to some people and not very common in the restaurant industry, which is sad.

Jill:
People almost expect if you're at all successful that you're not there, which is really counterintuitive. How do you expect to run a restaurant and be successful if you're not there? We do take time off, but if you're not consistently at your restaurant, I don't see how it could be successful long-term.

We've gained a lot of confidence in what some people thought was a strange idea: to do small plates.

Jessica:
Jill and I always say we have commitment issues. We can't commit to one big plate—we have to get like fifty different things to try it all.

Jill:
Every single city in the United States and in Europe does it. Why can't we? Why does Cleveland have to be twenty-five pounds of food on a plate for it to be a good meal? Small plates works, and it will continue to work because people are understanding it. Now different restaurants are calling themselves small plates or putting small plates on their menu, so it's catching on.

Jessica:
Some of the greatest people I've met in my life come through here. I've gained amazing relationships, Jill being one. We make great partners because we stay out of each other's lane. We don't micromanage each other. We openly talk about a lot of stuff that happens. We openly apologize if we make mistakes. We ask each

other questions. I'm a lot of hyperness, whereas Jill is not. Since opening this place, I've gained a level of calmness because she doesn't feed into my hyperness.

Every ten weeks, the entire restaurant menu changes. She tries all my cocktails, and I try all her food. We tell each other the truth and make adjustments. I also try really hard to do a wine list that pairs well with her food menu.

Jill:
It's mutual respect for what we both do here. That's it. We can get on each other's nerves—there's no such thing as a perfect relationship. But people are always shocked at how well we get along.

Success is being able to pay your bills, your staff, and yourself. It's being able to walk out of this restaurant nightly or daily and know that you did a good job. It's being able to take days off and not stress out.

What is "success"?

Jill:
Success is being able to pay your bills, your staff, and yourself. It's being able to walk out of this restaurant nightly or daily and know that you did a good job. It's being able to take days off and not stress out. Everybody here treats this place like it's theirs, which is something that we've tried to instill from day one: it's not about us, it's about all of us. If we're successful, you're successful.

Jessica:
I love it, love it, love it when guests come in here and are not really sure. "Am I going to like this? This is weird. I don't even know what this is—I have to Google everything." And I can confidently tell them to just sit back, relax, enjoy their evening, and let their server handle it. Grown men have walked out of here in tears, thanking

us. To me, that's success—giving people an experience.

A lot of people think that as owners, we're making a ton of money. I have a friend who doesn't understand why I come to work so early. I have orders to do, I have to go to the bank, I have liquor to pick up, I have a meeting with a wine rep. Jill has nine hours of prep to do before we open. They fantasize that we're just sitting at the bar drinking. I think that's a huge misconception, not just for us but across the board.

Jill:
Some people don't understand why something costs as much as it does. It should be mandatory in high school to work in a restaurant so everyone can understand how much work it takes to get one plate on your table.

Jessica:
What you bought out of a can at the grocery store, we got out of the ocean yesterday.

How do restaurants shape the Cleveland community?
Jill:
Restaurants are gathering places and second homes to a lot of people. We're the reason you get out of your house. If you don't want to cook, we're here. If you need a drink after a long day, we're here. We're everything. We're party planners, we're the dinner dates, we're the first dates.

You can make a career out of working front of house, and there's nothing to be ashamed of about it at all. There's a huge stigma about that.

WE SAW EVERYTHING THERE IS TO SEE IN THE RESTAURANT INDUSTRY. WE BROUGHT WITH US THE GOOD STUFF, AND WE KNOW WE'RE NOT GOING TO TOLERATE THE BAD STUFF.

Best piece of advice

Jessica:
You can make a career out of working front of house, and there's nothing to be ashamed of about it at all. There's a huge stigma about that. With back of house staff, just because you went to school doesn't mean you can cook, and it doesn't mean you deserve to make $100,000 a year.

Jill:
I didn't go to culinary school. I still don't know how to cook. I think there was a huge swell of humans going to culinary school because they wanted to be famous chefs when the Food Network came out. But that's not reality. People need to check their ego and just put their head down and work. Write shit down. Learn from the people around you. Ask questions. Try to move up. Be able to handle constructive criticism. If you're a sensitive person, you shouldn't work in this business.

Jessica:
I didn't go to college. We grew up in the day when you put your head down, shut your mouth, and paid very close attention to the good, the bad, and the ugly. That's one of the reasons we're successful—we saw everything there is to see in the restaurant industry. We brought with us the good stuff, and we know we're not going to tolerate the bad stuff.

Why Cleveland?

Jessica:
I was born and raised here. My husband got transferred to Detroit, and I moved there for a very long two-and-a-half years. As soon as I could get back, I put our house on the market the next day and moved. It's home. We love Lakewood. We love the community here.

Jill:
Cleveland is a cool spot. There are a lot of great things here—our museums, our beachfront, the growing restaurant scene, and the cost of living.

Jessica:
The Metroparks and walking and biking and hiking. There's no reason not to live here.

An ideal picture of Cleveland

Jill:

I would like to have winning sports teams. Not that I'm into sports at all, but it helps the economy by leaps and bounds. I would like to see more restaurants doing cooler shit and pushing the envelope instead of what they think people want. I would like to see more sunshine.

Cleveland has progressed and regressed so many times in the twenty-six years I've been an adult here, with certain areas and gentrification. As many people who move in, other people who have been here for a long time get pushed out. It's important to rejuvenate cities and try to thoughtfully bring people into them.

MALAZ ELGEMIABBY

Interdisciplinary designer and
founding principal of ELMALAZ

Malaz Elgemiabby is an award-winning interdisciplinary designer who develops building plans that truly respond to people's needs. Her landmark project in Cleveland is Ohio City's Riverview Welcome Center. She worked with many community partners to transform a near-dormant community center into a meaningful gathering space for programming and events that will be integrated into the long-term vision for an Irishtown Bend park. In 2019, she was the designer in residence for Cleveland Foundation Creative Fusion and launched her own consultancy firm, ELMALAZ.

The beginning

I always wanted to be a mother. Every time I was asked, "What do you want to be?" I would say, "A mother" and my father would say, "No, a doctor!" I accepted that I would be a doctor. Everyone kept calling me "Dr. Malaz" and saying I'd be the first female doctor in the family. When it came time for me to choose a college, I got a scholarship at the age of fifteen—a very early age—for medical school. As soon as I went there, I realized it was not what I wanted to do.

Looking back, I realized I always wanted to be an architect when I was a kid—I was building little huts, converting old air-conditioning containers into a library, or creating other things. What initially inspired me to be an architect was the architect who designed our house. My mom is a single mother. She worked so hard to save money and build us a house, which is a huge accomplishment for a woman in Sudan. She hired an architect, and he built a house that we totally hated. He built the house without talking to us—not even one time. Sudan is a matriarchal society, so all of our lives revolved around being near my grandmother, who lived with us. She would sit in her room and we would all come sit with her, watch TV with her, eat next to her, and even bring our mattresses on the floor so we could sleep next to her. He built us a house with so many rooms, and we never slept in any of them. We always occupied the one small room that was supposed to be for my grandmother. If he had spoken to us or seen the way we lived our lives, he would have designed the house completely differently, and it wouldn't have been a waste of my mother's hard-earned money.

I studied for three years in medical school in Sudan at the University of Khartoum. Every year, I would go to my family and say, "I don't want to do this." One day I went to the architecture school and sat through their end-of-year presentation. When it was finished, I told myself, "I think I can be an architect." I kind of rebelled against my family and decided to move to London to study architecture. It was tough because I really had to fight everyone. No other woman in my family had ever left the country to study abroad. My family told me I wouldn't have money there. I said, "I will work," but I had never worked a day in my life at that age—I was only seventeen years old at the time.

My mom was a dreamer. She was one of the first businesswomen in Sudan. I thought if she could fight the whole society to become an independent, self-made entrepreneur, I should take the next step and go outside the country to face new challenges.

Growing up in London, alone

In London, everything was new, especially coming from a very insular, very conservative family. I felt free to think, imagine, and challenge myself. I felt like a whole person—not someone's daughter or sister, not someone's something. For the first time, I was myself. It was hard, but it was an amazing journey. I grew up in London. I started to understand who I was, what my values were, and what type of designer I wanted to be. The hard part was that I had to do all of it alone, but that was also the beauty of it. I survived it and became a better person as a result.

We need architecture to help build community rather than segregate it further, racially or socioeconomically.

I graduated from London Metropolitan University in 2010. I chose that program because it focuses on the impact of design on people's lives. I put a lot of effort into listening, observing how people actually function, and designing something that truly responds to people's needs. Many architects come with predetermined ideas about how you should do things. They don't allow themselves the opportunity to observe and learn. Sometimes you might observe that someone doesn't get the chance to sit down. So, you can create a design that would encourage people to take a break. Or, you may observe that they don't get to interact with each other; they're lonely. Then, you can create a design that responds to their real needs beyond just a shelter and a place to sleep.

At the time I graduated, it was the recession, so not many building projects were happening in London, but architecture was playing a very important role in growing cities in the Middle East. I was very curious about how to design for a community that doesn't yet exist. So I went to Qatar, worked there for a little bit, then did my master's degree at Virginia Commonwealth University.

Civic architecture

When I finished my degree in 2015, my mother fell sick and I decided to go back to Sudan. By that time, she had established a nonprofit organization called the Sudanese Business Women

Development Center. Its mission is to help Sudanese women overcome a lot of obstacles, like banks refusing to give women loans to start their businesses. I ran the organization for six months and learned a lot. I got to talk to women directly about their aspirations and how the environment often fails them. Building designs can limit their mobility. A lot of people design for single people or men, who can move anywhere. They don't design for women who have children. Access to transportation can be the difference between a woman being able to start work or not. Having a place that's well-connected to the services around them can be what allows a family to move from poverty to having a stable income.

> *A lot of people design for single people or men, who can move anywhere. They don't design for women who have children.*

The projects that really stand out to me are the ones that have a more civic practice approach, which means that I sit with the community first, then we come up with the idea, and I help execute it with my skill set. One of those was a Saturday market that women wanted to create in Sudan. The need for it came from the women themselves. It was a small project, just a 100,000-square-foot space. But it was very impactful. That small space has changed a lot of women's lives. It doesn't just serve them as a place to sell—it serves as a place for them to form a community of entrepreneurs who help each other. It's a place for women to gather and sell their products, feel safe, and bring their children. They took a lot of ownership because they were part of the design project from the beginning to the end.

Coming to Cleveland

When I came to Cleveland in 2016, I knew it was a city on the verge of change and was starting to be revived, with a lot of places going through gentrification. That's an issue that I really care about because it's where architecture impacts people's life in a very dramatic way—it moves people out of their houses or out of their neighborhoods altogether. Or it can bring new people and start new communities.

Malaz and her son at Hamilton Collaborative in St. Clair-Superior

DON'T BE AFRAID OF MAKING MISTAKES. YOU'RE GOING TO MAKE MISTAKES, YOU'RE GOING TO BE MISUNDERSTOOD, YOU'RE GOING TO SAY THE WRONG THING SOMETIMES. BUT THAT'S THE ONLY WAY YOU CAN LEARN.

So for Cleveland, the question is how can we do gentrification right? New buildings are nice, but low-income buildings have cheap builds, are not as well thought out, and don't really suit the people who live there. When you see that practice—that people don't deserve a good-quality building because they're poor or from a certain racial background—it aggregates a lot of issues that exist in the community. We need architecture to help build community rather than segregate it further, racially or socioeconomically. Many architects are afraid of doing that. They just ignore it or pretend it doesn't exist.

Riverview Welcome Center

In Cleveland, the Riverview Welcome Center was one of my favorite projects. For that project, I drove Uber and Lyft in the neighborhood so I could talk to people who wouldn't otherwise be able to attend planning meetings because they have two jobs or a family at home. I really wanted to understand how everybody experienced their neighborhood. Many of the people I talked to said they need a place to just be. They feel like they can't just be without having to pay money. Or people would say that they really like the diversity of the neighborhood and wish there were more things to do together. Some people needed a space that would be inclusive of them, regardless of their income. Other people with higher income found that they craved community but hadn't really connected with the community in a meaningful way because they were in their own silo.

I think the project was successful because we established four values, which were community, diversity, inclusivity of seniors and children—who have very few places catering to them, and dignity. I kept hearing that people felt they didn't have dignity in the neighborhood. I asked, "What does dignity mean?" It means being able to provide for their family. It means jobs in the neighborhood. It means that their basic human rights are taken care of. It means being seen—people look at them and recognize them as part of the community. That's what inspired the temporary photographs on the side of the building.

We created two visions. In the short-term vision, the building serves as a place to bring the community together and develop programming ideas. The long-term design vision is to create a viewing platform for downtown and the river that's accessible at any time of the day to everyone. It's going to be a free, open space for everyone to enjoy being in their city. We also want to create a community kitchen to link Ohio City Farm and the West Side Market to the building.

Another thing that we heard all the time was that the community wants a place that can tell our story—the history of this place—so we want to create a family-friendly museum that incorporates local art in a high-quality space. It's part of the bigger Irishtown Bend park development project taking place over the next four years. The location is so significant to all of Cleveland. This is going to be a landmark where people come to see Cleveland on the viewing deck and learn about the history of Cleveland. It's inclusive to everyone instead of just the people who can afford condos overlooking the river.

I have a lot of support for this project from the Cleveland Foundation, the Cuyahoga Metropolitan Housing Authority, local community development corporations, Ohio City Inc., the City of Cleveland public art department, Land Studio, and the Cleveland Clinic.

The ultimate project

Motherhood is the ultimate project in life. Sometimes our society is not geared to support working moms to create a balanced life. So I sacrificed a lot of time and energy in order to do everything. I'm grateful to my son for being so patient with me in coming with me to my meetings. What I've gained is a community. I moved into the Ohio City neighborhood. Before the Riverview Welcome Center project, I was lonely in a whole new country by myself. I missed my family, and I didn't know the optics of me being able to go back to my country because Sudan was put on the travel ban. I would risk being able to come back. Now I've gained a community, a sense of belonging, and people who love me, who stepped up and said, "We are your community," and I'm really grateful for that.

What's next?

Even though there's often the intention to engage with the community, many architecture practices are lacking the procedures and tools to achieve that. So I decided to do two things: teach those skills to the younger generation of architects at Kent State University, and start my own consultancy business, ELMALAZ, so I can help other architects engage in the community in a way that can drive a better design outcome and process.

I want to design the Sudanese cultural garden in Cleveland. But before that, we need to unite the two segregated Sudanese communities in Cleveland—we're about four hundred people in total. To bring them together, I'm converting a camper van into a mobile recording and photography studio to tell the stories of Sudanese refugees and immigrants who made Cleveland home. In August, we'll come together for Salam Day (Peace Day), where we're going to share our rich culture and history with the Cleveland community.

What is "success"?

Success for me is success for everyone. If I'm the only one succeeding in life, that's a failure.

Best piece of advice

Don't be afraid of making mistakes. You're going to make mistakes, you're going to be misunderstood, you're going to say the wrong thing sometimes. But that's the only way you can learn. Don't be afraid of new things. Don't be afraid of new people or people who are different from you. Don't be afraid to check your own biases that can influence your design.

An ideal picture of Cleveland

An ideal version of Cleveland is the Cleveland that takes care of its community and its most vulnerable. Someone as far away as Westlake cares about and will stand up for children being affected by lead poisoning in East Cleveland. I've lived in so many communities around the world, and I really think that Cleveland has a chance to do something great.

JULIA KUO

Illustrator

Julia Kuo creates thoughtful illustrations for projects ranging from greeting cards to public art. Her work has brought more than a dozen books to life—including *100 Days in Cleveland*—and has been featured in national publications, including *The New York Times*, *Buzzfeed*, and *Vice*.

Julia at Ohio City Galley in Ohio City

The beginning

Even though I always liked drawing, I never really thought I would make a career out of art. It was always that thing in the background. My parents ran a small business when I was growing up, and I think because of that I was always more practical.

I made sure to go to a college that had an art department and thought I would just minor in art. I actually took so many art classes during my freshman year that the art school said they would ban me from art classes if I didn't change my major. At the time, I was enrolled in the business school and thought I'd do something responsible with my life. I eventually double majored in art and business. Having that background has helped me know how to run a small business, take care of myself, and be professional. It took me a while to get enough validation from my professors, internships and some other things here and there to realize I was doing well enough that maybe I could do well outside of school as an illustrator.

Two-and-a-half magical years

I'm not from Cleveland; I came here for a job at American Greetings. It's hard to get full-time or in-house work as an illustrator, so getting that job while still in school was very validating. Working there was fun; it's where I met a lot of my best friends. I was a planner, which means that I designed the cards and someone else illustrated them, so I got a slightly higher-level view of how things happened. I was there for two-and-a-half very magical years. It was a low-responsibility time because I went into it with a very relaxed attitude.

I was also always thinking about doing my own thing. As an illustrator, or as a student becoming an illustrator, the goal is always to be a freelancer. That's kind of how you get the jobs that people always want. It's really scary to take that leap right out of school. So it makes sense to have a job, save money, and get some experience first.

Work begets work

Three girls from American Greetings and I started our own stationery company called The Nimbus Factory when we left our jobs. We made all sorts of paper goods—journals, cards, notepads. It was fun getting to make whatever you wanted, going to renegade craft fairs, and trying to sell things.

Illustration by Julia Kuo. Featured on a utility box at the corner of Payne Avenue and East 40th Street in Asiatown.

We had no issue with creating things and making them look beautiful. We ran into more challenges figuring out which direction to take things. Do we get a manager or try to do everything ourselves? Do we try to sell everything online or put in the labor and go to craft shows? At the same time, we were in our midtwenties and were all starting to figure out our own careers. Two of the girls were becoming moms at the same time, I was beginning my own freelance career, and another girl was interested in environmentalism, so producing lots of paper didn't fit with what she wanted in a career. Even though we continued to collaborate on other projects and are still friends, we realized that that particular business wasn't the right fit anymore and naturally went our own ways.

Even while working at American Greetings, I was starting to get freelance jobs here and there. By the time I left, I didn't have enough freelance income to support myself. I knew I just needed to take a leap of faith and that it would take a lot of time. I got lucky from there. Early on, I could literally trace each job to a job that came before it. I had been told that work begets work, but it was cool to experience it for myself. I was working all the time—I knew I'd have to work hard to make this career happen, and I expected those around me to understand that. In retrospect, I can see how the stress I felt from work permeated my relationships.

For my first chapter book, I did illustrations for Jenny Han's *Clara Lee and the Apple Pie Dream*. The important thing about that book is that it's how I met my agent. My agent represented the writer and asked if I wanted to work with her. At the time, I had no idea what an agent was worth, and now she's turned out to be a really big reason I'm still doing this. I'd say that books have accounted for about 50 percent of my work in the years since and are some of the more exciting projects I've received, so I'm really fortunate that she reached out to me.

Early on, I could literally trace each job to a job that came before it.

Getting outside and getting inspired

Illustration provides less of a mental challenge for me these days. It's a combination of sticking to it, working hard, good luck, and being open to opportunities. Once my career started to feel less tenuous, I got really obsessed with rock climbing, which pushes your mental and physical limits. I never knew I could be so obsessed with anything. It was nice to have these two things I really cared about: climbing and illustration. I started climbing small mountains in Denver, and this past August I climbed Mount Rainier. That was probably mentally the most difficult thing I've done, which is why I'm very proud of it. As an illustrator, it was the most gorgeous thing I've ever seen. And it's such a shame that it was so cold that I couldn't draw it.

I also did a residency at Banff National Park twice. I loved it because it blended illustration and fine art. Everyone else there was a fine artist, so during that residency I got to see how different those categories are and how differently we think. Being there was so inspiring. I have a very pragmatic approach to illustration because it's a business—there's a concept that I need to fulfill. Fine artists are so different in their pursuit of the craft. It's a much purer form of the medium. While it's not me, I still learned a lot from it.

My turn to give

Teaching was something I had always been curious about. As I got a little bit older, I felt like I had something to offer. It was exciting for it to be my turn to give. I tried out teaching the history of illustration at Columbia College Chicago for three or four years. Then I ended up going back to my alma mater, Washington University in St. Louis, and taught a semester there.

Having students was not as natural for me as I would have liked it to be, but it was still rewarding. A lecture can be prepared so tightly, but there's always going to be an element of unpredictability— you don't know how things are going to go or how your students are going to respond to it. It felt scary. I'm pretty proud for getting through it without any disasters.

I think it will be harder for me to work as an illustrator as an older person because illustration inherently favors trendy things—art directors feel a lot of pressure to hire illustrators who are doing something new. I imagine I'll go back to school myself, get a master's degree, then settle down and teach again later on in my career.

Art in Cleveland

On a superficial level, public art is a gift to your eyes to see on a regular basis. When a city has art, music, and cultural performing arts, it feels richer and more lived in, and that's when people start to be proud of it.

The artwork I created for the Asiatown utility box (pictured on page 82) is cool because my figure is Asian and she's doing something adventurous. Public art should never be dominated by one particular person—it should always be a wide array of different artists, and it naturally lends itself to that.

What is "success"?

Success is working hard enough to have your work exist somewhere in the world. It has to do with working really hard and with your work living apart from you and doing something on its own.

Illustration by Julia Kuo.

Best piece of advice

Be as prolific as you possibly can. There's nothing better you can do for yourself than to put as much of your work as possible out there for other people to see.

Be as prolific as you possibly can. There's nothing better you can do for yourself than to put as much of your work as possible out there for other people to see.

SUCCESS IS WORKING HARD ENOUGH TO HAVE YOUR WORK EXIST SOMEWHERE IN THE WORLD.

There's a phrase that my parents used to say in Chinese. To translate, it would be, "First bitterness, then happiness." I used to hate it because I wanted to do the opposite. But I guess that's what being an adult is—you have to do those things that you don't want to do, and then you can relax.

Why Cleveland?

Cleveland was very pivotal in understanding myself when I got out of college. I grew up in L.A., and I always thought I'd go back there or to a similarly big city. But once I came here, I made lots of friends, and there were so many contrasts to L.A. Here, people expect to get to know you. I was really touched by the way everyone wanted to invest.

In 2011, I decided to draw one thing I liked in Cleveland every day for one hundred days and post it. People liked it a lot, and I got attention for it in a way I had never received. I realized that's what you get from being in a smaller pond: if you give to the city, people will appreciate it. That was a very humbling thing to learn, and it made me appreciate smaller cities.

JODI BERG

President and CEO
of Vitamix

Jodi Berg has been at the helm of the fourth-generation family company Vitamix for more than ten years. But she'll tell you her higher calling is helping others connect to their own purpose as well as promoting the transformative power of whole, natural foods and all the delicious ways they can be prepared. Jodi turned the small company into a global brand by introducing the Vitamix in more than 140 countries and fostering a purpose-driven culture.

Jodi at the Vitamix corporate
headquarters in Olmsted Falls

The beginning

I was very blessed to have parents who let me dream about being anything I wanted to be. I went through a phase of wanting to be an astronaut and all sorts of other big, incredible things. I went to college to be an engineer, but within two semesters I realized I hated it. Within a very short period of time, I transferred to Bowling Green State University, fell into hospitality management, and realized that what I really wanted was to serve people and bring a smile to their face.

I ended up working at the Residence Inn in sales, and they would send me to properties that weren't doing well. I saw each property I went to as an incredible opportunity—not just in terms of bringing more guests to the hotel but also to turn the whole hotel entity into something that provides fulfillment for the people who stay there and work there. I didn't realize it at the time, but I was setting out to impact the culture of the different units I was working at.

Then I decided to get my MBA at Washington State University, and one of the classes I took was in quality. I absolutely fell in love with quality—getting to the root cause of an issue, fixing it, and seeing its potential. My uncle, who was the president of Vitamix at the time, was setting up a quality division. I asked him if I could help him for a while so I could explore this whole quality thing and understand what I wanted to do with it.

A passion for quality

The Ritz-Carlton in Cleveland had just won a Malcolm Baldrige National Quality Award. I realized that's what I wanted to do: bring my two loves together—quality and hospitality management. I watched the director of quality, Emily Yen, give a presentation about the Malcolm Baldrige Award, and I stood in a long line to talk to her afterward. I thought of all these intelligent, wonderful things I was going to say, but when I got to the front of the line, what came out of my mouth was, "Hi, my name is Jodi Barnard. I want your job." I was bumbling all over the place thinking nobody would hire me now—I can't even carry on a sentence. But when I finally took a deep breath, I explained that I just loved what she did. When I had opportunities, I would take her to lunch and learn from her. When Emily was promoted, I ended up getting my dream job as the director of quality at the Ritz-Carlton in Cleveland. I was a shoo-in for the job because I understood what she did and I had the passion.

When I'm passionate about something, I can talk about it easily. The vice president of quality for the Ritz-Carlton realized I liked public speaking, so when he wasn't available to give one of his presentations, he would send me. I got to travel all over the world talking about the Ritz-Carlton. That gave me wonderful exposure to international business. I realized I had a third love: hospitality, quality, and now I adored how big and amazingly beautiful this world is and how all the different cultures come together.

Quality is all about continuous improvement. In about two and a half years, I had improved things there such that they didn't need a full-time person in my position. I worked myself out of a job. About that same time, Vitamix was going international. I thought I could bring all my passions together, so I came back to Vitamix to head up our international division. I fell in love with it. Then my dad, who was president of Vitamix at the time, asked if I would oversee our household division. I was even more in love with the household division because it's changing people's lives—people who use the Vitamix are oftentimes literally transforming themselves from the inside out.

Gaining clarity in purpose

When I was thirty, I had an autoimmune disease that progressively got worse, and it couldn't be diagnosed. At one point, I was admitted to the hospital. My mom turned to the doctor and asked, "How long do you think she'll be in the hospital?" He turned his back to me, tried to lower his voice, and said, "Right now we're not even sure that we're going to get her out."

I hadn't even begun to live yet. I thought about all the time I might have wasted when I wasn't focused on what was really important. As I lay in the hospital and went through recovery, I made a decision that I was given a gift to have more time, and I wanted to make a difference. What came out of that moment for me was clarity about what matters. I know the difference the Vitamix can make in people's lives, and I know the value of our employees being connected to a brand that truly cares about their success. Because I know that's the destination, I have incredible clarity. I'm not going to do something unless it's a means to achieving my bigger purpose because time is so unbelievably precious. And you don't know that until you almost don't have any more.

You only have one life. All the amazing people who work for Vitamix put in anywhere from eight to ten to sometimes twelve hours a day. Those are hours they're never getting back. As a leader, my purpose is not about growing a company for the sake of growing. I see my purpose as helping everybody around me—customers, stakeholders, community—be able to say, "I did something, it was worth it, I mattered."

Noticing trends

While heading up the household division, I noticed a lot of different trends coming together at the same time. Around 2004, people were starting to eat differently. They were looking at why they eat and what they eat. People were thinking about whole food, natural, and organic. People were connecting the dots to the fact that food truly would impact how they feel today and possibly how they could feel tomorrow. I was encouraging all of us as a

company to figure out how to embrace that trend and become a brand that people can believe in.

When my great-grandfather started the company in 1921, he had a personal passion for helping people experience whole food in a healthy, delicious, simple way. The company didn't start with blenders—there weren't any back then. But he traveled around the country selling modern kitchen products like the can opener so people could have access to healthy produce all year round instead of only during the growing season. Times were changing enough that I thought this might be the opportunity my grandparents, great-grandparents, aunts, and uncles would have dreamed of. Maybe this was our time to reach more people and change more lives.

Becoming a global brand

One day, my dad called me into his office and shared with me that he was going to retire and that he wanted to find a replacement. I said, "That's fabulous. I'll help you because I want to make sure that whoever leads this company next has a vision that is at least as big as mine." He said, "I was thinking about you," which made me literally laugh hysterically. I was laughing so hard. I didn't know how to run a company. I'd never set out to run a company. That wasn't on my bucket list—that wasn't my goal. I told him the board would talk some sense into him. After multiple conversations, I was the one they actually talked some sense into. I realized that if what was really driving me was this desire to change lives and give people wings, then that was more important than knowing how to run a company. So I said yes, but I needed two years to prepare.

> *I realized that if what was really driving me was this desire to change lives and give people wings, then that was more important than knowing how to run a company.*

Coming into that role, I thought we needed to help change the way people think about whole foods once and for all. The challenge was that we were still so small that another blender company could have taken as much money as we would have made in an entire year in revenue and dumped it into product development and marketing toward health food trends. Other companies could have seen this opportunity coming and taken advantage of it. The only reason I saw it first is:

1) Those companies are big, and it's harder to see things when you're big.

2) I was so focused on helping people think differently about food and making healthy food delicious that when these trends started happening, I couldn't help but notice.

People sometimes call that a gut instinct or intuition, but I think it's a matter of understanding the end game—knowing your purpose and what you're trying to achieve. We needed to create a brand that would encourage people to be able to make the choices they need to make. I had no idea how to do that. The only thing I knew was that when I'm focused on my own personal purpose, you can't stop me. I can work 24/7. I can overcome perceivably unattainable obstacles. I know what decisions to make because I'm focused on that bigger picture.

I thought if that works for me, I need to make it possible for everyone in the entire company to have a personal connection to what we're trying to do. I wanted each of them to get out of bed because they have a personal purpose they want to achieve, and they get to live that personal purpose by coming to work. It's a synergistic win. That's how we went from being a pretty small company to a global brand.

A million challenges

There are a million challenges every single day. We're the cutting edge of blending technology. We have hundreds and hundreds of patents. Those are all challenges because if you're doing something that's never been done before, sometimes it's going to work, and sometimes it's not.

We also have challenges with creating and maintaining a culture where people can truly be empowered to live their personal purpose, especially when we're always infusing our organization with people from work cultures that are so opposite of that. With new employees, it's a challenge to help people realize that we truly mean it when we say we want them to know their purpose and help them figure out how to achieve it, and that they truly matter and are not a number.

When the company was growing, I was also raising my daughters. Between being a working mom and trying to be there for my family, plus the employees, plus the customers, plus the community, plus anyone else who needed me to be there—I'd say my biggest regret is that I would have wanted more of the quiet times with my daughters. Fortunately I still have time.

Through my work, I've met amazing, unbelievable people—I've had opportunities to have very personal moments with people and in different places around the world. I get to feel good about

TIME IS SO UNBELIEVABLY PRECIOUS. AND YOU DON'T KNOW THAT UNTIL YOU ALMOST DON'T HAVE ANY MORE.

what I'm doing. I get to feel peace and joy. Now, if I were to pass, I wouldn't have the regrets that I did when I was thirty.

Being a woman leader has its perks

Don't look at something as a challenge because you're a woman. That may be why something is happening; that may be why a challenge exists. Think about how to overcome it creatively and how you can actually get farther along in the situation because you're a woman. If we only focus on the challenges of gender, we're not paying attention to the opportunities.

When I first set out in international business, it was 1997. On one trip, I was meeting a potential distributor in Japan by myself. My objective was to convince him that our product was right for him to carry. It was very traditional at the time for a Japanese company to put a potential partner through the rigors of asking a bunch of questions, then taking them out drinking in the evening. They didn't know what to do with a woman—they couldn't ask me the same types of questions. The first day I was at their offices, I was sitting in a room with seven to ten men, and we weren't getting anywhere. It was awkward and uncomfortable all day long.

If we only focus on the challenges of gender, we're not paying attention to the opportunities.

At dinner, they took me to a beautiful restaurant overlooking Tokyo. I sat directly across from the president of the company, and he had all the men in black suits sitting on each side of him. We really just needed to get to know each other personally, but they had no idea what to do with me as a woman. There were folded napkins in front of us. Drawing on everything I knew about the culture, the gentleman I was sitting across from, and how awkward the day was, I picked up the napkin and said, "Oh look—it's a hat" and put the napkin on my head. I knew that in Japanese culture, they won't allow somebody to lose face, especially a woman. So, the eyes of the gentleman across from me got as big as saucers, and he picked up his napkin and put it on his head, too.

All the people he brought with him looked at him, panicked, looked at me, reached down, and stuck their napkin on their head. I said, "Do you have any idea how silly we look?" He looked around and realized that I knew it wasn't a hat. But now everyone had it on their head. I started chuckling, he started to bust a gut laughing, and as soon as he was allowed to laugh, everyone was allowed to laugh, and we just laughed until tears rolled down our faces. Then we could have a real conversation and get to know each other.

That was incredibly risky. If I were a man, no way would I have gotten away with that. But because I was female, I knew about the culture, I knew the president was a family man who loved to be silly, and I knew they were just as uncomfortable as I was, I saw it as a way to break the ice. Later on, I was able to say that I'd had enough to drink so I could keep my wits about me the whole evening, which a man could not have done in 1997. When I was tired, I was able to thank him for a lovely evening and go back to my hotel room—a man could never have done that. As he walked me out to put me in a taxi to go back, he shook my hand and told me we were going to do a lot of amazing business together.

What is "success"?

One particular testimonial letter sticks out in my mind. A mom wrote us sharing that she started feeding her daughter—who had to be fed through a feeding tube since birth—whole, natural foods processed in the Vitamix. It was smooth enough that it wasn't clogging the feeding tube, and her daughter was getting whole-food nutrition. The mom shared a picture of her daughter before and after—in the "after" picture, she was running outside with friends, her eyes were sparkling, and she had all this energy. The mom wrote, "Thank you, thank you, thank you. You have given our entire family a new lease on life in an incredible way."

I shared this testimonial with employees so they would know they're truly impacting people's lives. I noticed one of the employees was tearing up. Afterward, she said, "As you were reading that, I realized I might have been the one who built the machine that changed that child's life." That's what success looks like: when you have a customer who's achieving their goals and an employee who feels really good about the fact that they're changing someone's life.

Why Cleveland?

My great-grandparents moved Vitamix to Cleveland—we didn't start here. When they came to Cleveland for the Great Lakes Exposition in 1936 and 1937, the story goes that they decided these were the most dedicated, hardest-working people they ever met, and they wanted to have their company in Cleveland. I have to agree with them. We have unbelievable people here.

An ideal version of Cleveland

My ideal Cleveland is more diverse. We'd come together and share our knowledge and expertise to make this an amazing place for everyone. We'd be reaching our hands down to anyone in our beautiful, amazing community who didn't have advantages or opportunities to overcome their challenges. As a community and as a city, we would benefit tremendously from doing that.

JASMIN SANTANA

Cleveland City
Councilwoman,
Ward 14

Jasmin Santana is a people investor. After a close and contentious race against the twelve-year incumbent of Ward 14, she became the first Latina elected to Cleveland City Council. Now, her efforts are focused on developing the Clark-Fulton and Stockyards neighborhoods in a way that's equitable for the residents who have lived there for years.

Jasmin in her office in the
Clark-Fulton neighborhood

The beginning

Growing up, I always felt I wanted to do something big. I didn't know what. I would see myself being a motivational speaker or someone who would impact people and change lives. Or, I wanted to be a preacher and make speeches geared toward spirituality and health. That's always been my dream—developing people. I saw myself working specifically with women.

I grew up in the Detroit-Shoreway. It was very blighted with lots of crime—very similar to the Clark-Fulton neighborhood now. My mom came from Puerto Rico, and she didn't even have to speak English because most of the corner stores, neighbors, and organizations spoke her language since there was a high population of Latinos. When that community started developing, we were forced to move, so I ended up in Ward 14 when I was fourteen years old. We grew up very independent but with a lot of struggles and challenges. I witnessed cycles of domestic violence. Women from this neighborhood experience a lot of trauma. At that time, I hated my childhood. But today I'm grateful for that journey because I learned so much from it. In my position now, I'm able to relate to people and families who are going through what I have already been through.

I was always involved in community engagement with the residents, and health has been my primary focus. For about nine years I worked at MetroHealth, which is an anchor institution here in the neighborhood. We had a lot of minority women presenting with late-stage breast cancer. To address this, we helped develop a community outreach program called Breasts and Amigas, which is still going on. The program has helped many women identify early-stage breast cancer because we meet them where they're at. We did health fairs, brought the Mammovan and doctors to do breast exams, and connected residents to forty organizations offering wraparound services.

Going grassroots

In my community engagement roles, I was working hard to change lives household by household, woman by woman. But to bring some transformation to our neighborhood, we needed someone in a leadership position to be at the table at city hall. I thought, *Who better than a woman and a Latina to represent her community?* So I ran for city council against a twelve-year incumbent. It was the ugliest race in Cleveland. Some men in the neighborhood were just not ready for a woman to be in leadership; they always imagined a man in that position. Another thing is that I wasn't as political; I didn't know anything about politics. I'm ordinary—a mom, daughter, sister—just a girl in the neighborhood wanting to make a difference.

To bring some transformation to our neighborhood, we needed someone in a leadership position to be at the table at city hall. I thought, "Who better than a woman and a Latina to represent her community?"

It was very intimidating. I had a lot of sleepless nights. Canvasing a lot gave me the power to overcome my fear. The more I spoke to families, the more I was reminded of why I was running. I kept hearing the same struggles and challenges that made me believe all my effort was worth it. I thought, *If I'm going to be able to help these families have a park down the street, own a house, put their kids in better schools, make sure material is translated for Spanish speakers...I have to keep going. I can't give up.*

From all my years working in the neighborhood, I developed a base of residents who knew my work with cancer, health disparities, lead issues, and women's empowerment. I also sold Mary Kay, so I was very well connected. I was always working behind the scenes to use my platform to help empower women and bring resources to the neighborhood. Most houses I canvased at, people remembered that I had helped them with a mammogram or when they didn't have health insurance and were excited to see me running. It was a spiderweb effect everywhere we went.

Equitable development

For me, equitable development means preparing the residents who are here. It's important for them to be at the table when decisions are made because oftentimes when a community does not get investment and things start getting worse, people just move. They move from this place they grew up in—their foundation. We invite and welcome with open arms people from the outside community. We want mixed-income housing. We want more diversity in our

MOST HOUSES I CANVASED AT, PEOPLE REMEMBERED THAT I HAD HELPED THEM WITH A MAMMOGRAM OR WHEN THEY DIDN'T HAVE HEALTH INSURANCE AND WERE EXCITED TO SEE ME RUNNING.

neighborhood. But the residents who have lived here their whole lives have to be the ones who decide what plans we are going to move forward with. They have nowhere to go after this, so the development must reflect their challenges.

For me, equitable development means preparing the residents who are here.

We want to make sure we're rehabbing and building homes that residents can afford so they can stay in the neighborhood rather than be priced out. We need a good school system. We need parks and green space. Culturally, we love to be with our families, so we need a gathering place to take them on a Saturday or Sunday. And, of course, safety is huge. That's going to take building relationships between police officers, stakeholders, and residents so they're talking to each other more.

The first year as a city councilwoman, I was lost. There were no goals, no vision for this ward. There was no playbook, no GPS of how I was going to move forward. A lot of key organizations had new leadership entering at the same time, and many of us had lived here our whole lives. With all the development that's happening, we decided we needed a master plan to make sure residents are not displaced and we're not gentrifying the neighborhood. Uniting all these organizations under a master plan is crucial before any funds are allocated for new programming or development. The plan involves talking directly to the current residents to capture an in-depth look at their needs. We want them to feel a sense of ownership and that they have a voice. That to us is so important.

We can develop all the bricks-and-mortar we want. But if you don't develop the people and prepare them to move into these storefronts and be ready to open their businesses or afford a home, we'll never thrive. So I'm a people investor—that's where my energy goes. Then I partner with organizations that are bricks-and-mortar and with financial investors.

Peaks and valleys

As soon as I became an elected official, some people who supported me started to think I'm a politician, a bad guy. Maybe

because they don't have full trust in the system, they think I'm going to forget why I ran in the first place. It's hard for me to be involved in the same way I was as a community engagement coordinator, so people think I've changed. That's not the case. My goals are still the same, and my vision is still the same. It prioritizes the residents of this neighborhood.

I've sacrificed my private life and a lot of time with my kids and my husband as a result of working very late hours. Time with friends. My social life. I've sacrificed a whole lot. I've put myself in the limelight. Now wherever I go, people are looking at what I'm doing. But I've gained courage. I've gained a network of colleagues whom I'm learning from on a daily basis, who impact me personally and professionally. I can see myself moving into something bigger down the line because of all these personal tools I'm gaining. I feel more confident.

For a long time, I was looking for something that seemed to be missing in my life. Now I feel like I'm where I need to be—I have this

sense of fulfillment. It's what gets me up in the morning; it's this fire that burns inside of me. No matter what the sacrifice is, at the end of the day I am so happy with what I do.

What is "success"?

I struggle with that—how do I know that I'm being successful? If I can help bring partners together and bring peace among organizations for the betterment of our neighborhood, that to me is success. If I can keep families in the neighborhood and they can be happy where they live, that to me is success. I am very proud to be called the convener and the peacemaker of this area. I'm proud because it's been very hard to bring people together, and I have been able to do that.

Also, as the first Latina elected to Cleveland City Council, I feel a responsibility to create a sense of ownership and place for the Latino community. We don't have that citywide. You have Slavic Village, Asiatown...so many cultures represented in the city—but not Latinos. We don't even have a cultural garden. There is a lack of Latino representation all across the city. And Latinos are the highest foreign population.

Best piece of advice

We women have to speak a certain way, we have to look a certain way, we have to do the right things and be careful what we say—it's a lot of pressure. I would say to women, just be yourself. When I was able to just be myself and be genuine and honest, that's when I started being successful.

If you want go down a similar path to mine, get mentally prepared. Take care of yourself physically—eat healthy. Develop a support group. You're going to need your family and friends more than ever. You're going to be tired, and you're going to want to give up in the middle of that race. You're going to cry. You're going to scream. It's going to be ugly. But it's going to be well worth it. I don't think any leader hasn't been through something ugly. Embrace all your failures and learn from them.

An ideal picture of Cleveland

My ideal Cleveland would have a lot of businesses. You can take public transportation everywhere. You can take your family to eat at a restaurant at a reasonable price. You can walk on a nice sidewalk with trees, greenery, and flowers. And you're surrounded by healthy people. The opioid crisis is at its worst. The lead crisis is at its worst. If we can improve on the health commission of our city, that's the Cleveland I envision.

I choose to do my work here because I was born and raised in Cleveland. Cleveland has a lot of families. It's affordable. You can buy a big, huge house and live comfortably. It has the four seasons. It's very diverse, and there's just so much potential. And we live by a lake—there aren't a lot of states that are right by a lake. Traffic isn't out of hand like other cities. People are social. We have a little bit of everything here.

JACKIE WACHTER

Cofounder and
creative director
of FOUNT

Jackie Wachter and her husband, Phillip Wachter, started
FOUNT in 2014 out of a shared interest in sewing and
making things by hand. By focusing on creating quality,
long-lasting, ethically sourced bags and accessories,
they have quickly grown the leather goods company
into an iconic brand beloved by Clevelanders as well as
national and international customers.

Jackie at Fount's Asiatown studio

The beginning

As a young child, I loved to get dressed. In the morning, I'd wake up and just couldn't wait to pick out my outfit. I was always trying weird things with my style, even when I was little. My grandma taught me the basics of sewing. We started by making pillowcases, and then she taught me how to alter clothing.

I was always starting fake businesses. I had a jewelry business out of my locker in seventh grade until it got shut down by the principal. My sister and I *lived* for lemonade stands in the summer, and we sold handmade puppets. In college, I had a cleaning service, then designed jewelry boards. I've always loved making things and seeing if people wanted them.

After college, I spent six months in Liberia, which inspired me to go to fashion design school with the intention of starting a fair trade company. But I got down on myself about my goals and my purpose, and I got into a rough relationship that wasn't supportive of my being in fashion design. So I dropped out. I lost confidence in myself as a designer. I didn't have a natural eye for detail in sewing. I was very good at coming up with ideas, but executing them was hard for me, and I saw that as a barrier. Then I became a teacher for six years.

Jumping in headfirst

When I met my husband, Phillip, we started making things together just for fun. For Christmas the first year we were dating, I made him a laptop case and a pencil case out of boiled wool. When I gave him the gifts, he loved them and said, "Wouldn't this be so awesome if it were made out of leather?" We started researching how to sew leather on YouTube. Then we found this local place where we could buy leather, and they taught us some hand-tool methods, so we started hammering and sewing things by hand. After coming up with a few wallet and necklace designs, we gave them to our friends and family, who suggested we try to make a purse next.

We went to Amish country and bought an industrial World War II sewing machine that had been used to sew parachutes. We got it off of Craigslist for $200. The motor had died and been replaced with a lawn mower motor, so you couldn't control the speed. It had no backstitch; it was just superpowered. It was super hard to sew on—we called it Ferdinand the Bull—but that's what we used to make the first purse. I used to sell vintage at the Cleveland Flea, so we started to test our wallets, necklaces, and bags at the market. Everything sold. We listened to customer feedback and brought back new bags the next month.

I've been such a dreamer my whole life. We thought we could build a business from the very minute we made the first bag. We were just having so much fun with it. Phillip always had make-believe businesses as a kid, too. He designed his own Beanie Babies in fifth grade and sold them at his locker. In college, he wanted to start a denim company. When we met, our energies surged together. After a few months, we were only selling like seven bags per month, but we had both already decided to quit our jobs and jump in headfirst.

> *I've been such a dreamer my whole life. We thought we could build a business from the very minute we made the first bag.*

Within three months of taking that leap, we were featured in *Country Living* magazine. When the issue came out in October, our team grew from the two of us to nine of us to fulfill the hundreds of orders placed. Christmas came and went, but then in January we only sold two bags. My biggest fear was that we were going to have to lay people off, so we decided to start traveling around the country to find more markets like the Cleveland Flea.

For years, we sewed during the week and traveled to shows over the weekend. Then we had a baby, and he would come with us. I'd carry him in a carrier while selling the bags, or he'd be in a Pack 'n Play next to me while we were sewing. At a certain point, that stopped working—our son wanted to crawl all over the place and the studio was just not a safe place for a baby. Not to mention, I could hardly get anything done.

Then we got asked to be on the TV show *Cleveland Hustles*. It was funny because we had never wanted to open a store, but that was the prize for being one of the winners. We would never have opened a store otherwise, but it's been the biggest gift because it has helped us grow to a new level without having to travel every weekend.

An abundant source of desirable quality

I loved vintage bags, but the straps would always break and the linings would always get nasty and shred. When we started Fount, we decided to design an indestructible strap and never use lining. We've now sold thousands and thousands of bags and have never had a single strap break. In fact, we filled a bag full of cinder blocks and hung it on a hook for several weeks, and it was fine.

The meaning of the word *fount* is "an abundant source of desirable quality." That's our goal as a company: to make things that are quality over quantity. They are expensive bags, but we're using some of the finest ethically sourced leather and brass you can buy. We make everything here in our Cleveland studio, pay fair wages, and are striving to have a work culture that's really healthy and

that people love being a part of. We want our goods to be passed on through generations rather than ending up in landfills.

We're also starting to have a pulse on making sure that our impact on the world goes beyond making pretty bags. We're working to reduce our carbon footprint by composting our leather scraps and working with a tannery that purifies the water after they tan the hides. We plant trees with every purchase. We're using a by-product of the meat industry and giving it new life.

"How do you do it all?"

A lot of people ask me, "How do you do it all?" I don't do it all. We had a mountain of laundry that was washed but not folded and not in drawers for years. If you needed a T-shirt, you went to find it

WE WANT OUR GOODS TO BE PASSED ON THROUGH GENERATIONS RATHER THAN ENDING UP IN LANDFILLS.

in the pile. A year ago, I definitely burned out. I just didn't have any more to give. I sacrificed a lot of time with my kids. A goal of mine this year is to get better about that. It's not easy. I try to practice presence so that no matter where I am—in a meeting or at home with my kids—I'm 100 percent there. Before, I might have been playing cars with my son while thinking about an email I forgot to send. Now when I'm home, I put my phone away and say I'm not going to answer any messages until tomorrow.

Some people say that they think I'm fancy, but I'm just pretend fancy. Nearly all of my clothes are from thrift stores, second hand shops, or ethical brands—I'm going on seven years of being fast fashion–free. Our bags are also not fancy. They're meant to be your everyday durable bag. We had a customer who drove over her bag with her car—she left it on top like you leave your coffee. We conditioned it, and it looked brand new. Our bags are more expensive than a bag at Target and perhaps even Nordstrom, but they are meant to last a lifetime.

With Fount, it has been so cool to develop endurance because I have to stick with it through the highs and lows and ups and downs of business. My whole life had lacked commitment. I'm quick to get into things, but I have a hard time sticking with them. I was always trying new sports, I moved apartments every single year, I got new jobs every two years. I was addicted to change my whole life. I loved the beginning of things. This is the first thing I've ever stuck with this long. To be honest, I need to constantly remind myself that it's worth it to stick with it through the hard seasons. The first few years we had to live on a supertight budget. We always paid ourselves last. That was really challenging, but it taught me so much.

Start with what's in your hand

For anyone who wants to start something, start with what's in your hand. Sometimes people are looking to start something that's brand new to them, but your purpose might be doing the thing you're already doing to your greatest potential. Things that look like overnight successes are often actually the result of what people have been doing their whole lives. People see the harvest, but they don't see the groundwork of clearing the weeds and tilling the soil. You have to be a little crazy to start a business. This is more work than I ever imagined. It's crazy hours, and it's a lot of risk over and over again. You feel like you're jumping off cliff after cliff after cliff. You have to have goals—goals that you've written down and planned on and spoken out loud or journaled about. Be flexible with those goals, knowing that they might change and that it's okay to pivot.

Why Cleveland?

I love Cleveland. I long to see Cleveland the way my grandma and great-grandma saw it back in their day. It's exciting that it feels as though there is a renaissance happening in Cleveland. It's big enough to give you awesome opportunities, but it's small enough that people know each other and help each other out. It's a cool vibe. Our first studio cost $800 a month. It was rough around the edges, but we could have never done that in Chicago or New York. In my opinion, Cleveland has everything but a mountain.

Sometimes people are looking to start something that's brand new to them, but your purpose might be doing the thing you're already doing to your greatest potential.

An ideal picture of Cleveland

I'd love to see our next mayor turn Burke Lakefront Airport into a giant beach, expand the lakefront to reach from the East Side to the West Side, and add bike trails. It would be amazing—the lakefront could be the shining gem of Cleveland.

AHLAM ABBAS

Founder and CEO
of Dirty Lamb

When Ahlam Abbas has a dream, she makes it happen. In the time span of a few years, she became a model, then a nurse, then launched a natural, plant-based skin care line called Dirty Lamb, which is a play on her nickname, Lam. Her products are in TJ Maxx and Marshalls stores as well as subscription boxes and are also sold direct to consumers on the Dirty Lamb website.

The beginning

When I was little, I'd always say, "I'm the boss" while bagging groceries or helping out at my dad's grocery store, Roush's Market. At around five years old, I said I was going to be a baby nurse like my cousin. I had my mind set on that and ended up making it a reality.

Middle school was the worst. I felt like I didn't fit in, and I would try anything to fit in. That's when I started looking at models in magazines and thinking about how cool it would be to have such a glamorous job. I wanted to do it all—I can get bored easily and wanted to make sure I had an exciting life.

In high school, I earned my nurse technician license, then found a job at Barberton Hospital. Through that job, someone offered me the opportunity to take care of an elderly couple, which is still the best job I've ever had. They were the most positive, loving couple despite the health issues they were dealing with. That was an amazing experience, and it really pushed me to go into nursing.

While going through nursing school at The University of Akron, I modeled for MC2, an agency in Miami. People think it's superficial, but modeling helped me gain confidence, hustle, and a go-getter attitude. It pushed me to another level because I had to put myself in the most uncomfortable situations. My first casting was in New York for a Target ad. I walked in, saw hundreds of models waiting in line, and thought there was no way I would get the job since there were more experienced models. They didn't seem impressed with me at all, but I got a call back that week saying that I got the job. It showed me I can do anything. I still model sometimes for The Talent Group in Cleveland, which connects me to fun commercial jobs for things like jewelry and furniture.

Skin care is food

Throughout high school, I dealt with breakouts all the time. I wasn't satisfied with any product I tried. They always made my skin worse, and I was surprised that a lot of my go-to products had harmful ingredients in them. In college, my breakouts were still an annoyance. I would drag my feet to dermatologists because I wasn't comfortable in my own skin, and they'd recommend solutions that would make my skin worse at first. But who wants that?

*Your skin is your largest organ,
and it absorbs everything you put
on it, so I believe that skin care
should be thought of as food.*

Your skin is your largest organ, and it absorbs everything you put on it, so I believe that skin care should be thought of as food. When you eat plant-based foods, you see wonderful benefits, and it's the same thing when you use them topically. I started making skin care products for myself by researching which plants would be good for the problems I was dealing with and mixing a lot of Middle Eastern ingredients that I found in my kitchen.

My grandma was a big believer in natural remedies. And my dad told me that when he was in Palestine and someone had a cut or was even bleeding out but didn't have money to go to a doctor, they would pack the wound with Turkish coffee, and it would stop the bleeding and also heal the scar. I found that really interesting.

I had tried out different store-bought coffee scrubs but thought I could make a better one. That was my first product—a multiuse coffee scrub you can use on your face or body. It did all the things I wanted it to, like take away my skin's oiliness but still keep it hydrated, remove dead skin, and reduce acne and inflammation.

At first, I wasn't thinking of turning it into a business. I had friends and family trying it out and was getting really good feedback. When I told some of my friends in Florida about my coffee scrub, they invited me to set up a booth at Model Volleyball Miami Beach. At the booth, I set up a shower for both women and men to try the coffee scrub so I could get live feedback from people I didn't know. I also gave out free samples. People were really into it because it was so interactive. That gave me the confidence to believe I could really do something with it. I was envisioning what it could be but kept it as my side passion because I was still in school and then working as a nurse.

Ahlam at Akron Coffee Roasters, where she sources the coffee for some of her skin care products

Now or never

When I graduated, I started off working on the medical-surgical floor at Cleveland Clinic Akron General. It wasn't my first choice, but you have to take what you can get at the beginning of a nursing career. It was the worst experience—I can't say anything great about it. I kept thinking to myself, *Why did I go to school for this?* It was something I knew I had to get out of. One of the other nurses told me I should apply for the job that I really wanted on the neonatal intensive care unit floor. I had only been there a year and thought only nurses with the highest seniority got those jobs, but she said I should still apply.

I ended up getting my dream job on the NICU floor, and it was awesome. Being around new life was such a positive experience compared to my previous job. I was so happy, my coworkers were amazing, and we had the best time together. I couldn't

ask for anything more. But I still had my side project in my head. It occurred to me that if I wanted to do it, it was now or never. I decided I could always go back to nursing, and I'd rather take a risk than have regrets.

I decided I could always go back to nursing, and I'd rather take a risk than have regrets.

Launching Dirty Lamb

I attended a convention called Fear Paradox and learned from women around the world who all basically said, "What do you have to lose? Just do it. What's the worst that can happen?" That pushed me to launch Dirty Lamb at Indie Beauty Expo in New York. I wanted to launch with more than one product, so I literally made four new products three weeks before the show. My booth was set up on a very low budget. It cost me way more for my pass to go to the show. To catch people's attention, I just used a lot of green and had fun with it. My logo is a lamb, so it tends to pull people in.

I met the buyer for TJ Maxx and Marshalls when she visited my booth. We later continued our conversation over a phone meeting, and I sent her products for her team to test out. Then she started out with a small test order of roughly 1,200 units of the five SKUs I had. Two months later, I had an order and quit my job. After launching at that show and getting the retail account, I knew I couldn't give 100 percent to my job as a nurse with a full-time business.

The second time I did Indie Beauty Expo, I made a connection with a subscription box called FabFitFun. After about three months of following up and calling and emailing them, I finally confirmed an order, and I'm continuing to work with them. Dirty Lamb products have been featured as an add-on item, but my goal is to be a part of their big box, which would require millions of units. It's a matter of continuing to build my team and growing my brand to another level.

Building a brand

I've been so blessed that my brother, Rafat, owns a manufacturing and fulfillment center in Akron called Jetpack. In college, I would help them out with anything they needed and started to learn about their processes. They helped onboard Dirty Lamb and allowed me to manufacture and fulfill with them, so I was really lucky in that aspect.

For packaging and marketing, I made everything really cost-efficient at first because the business needed to make money. People often want to be perfect, even at first, but it doesn't work like that; you have to start from somewhere. Now that it's been a few years, I'm getting to the fun part because I'm doing a major rebrand in 2020. I'm very into sustainability and am hoping to add some refillable packaging and 100 percent recyclable glass containers. I'm almost taking a step backward with this rebrand in order to reach higher-end retailers like Sephora and Ulta. I want Dirty Lamb to be a handmade brand that's able to reach the masses.

Because of the fact that I'm using all-natural ingredients, it was a low barrier to enter the skin care world and start making my own products. Many people think you have to be a chemist or have years of school to start, but that's not the case anymore. If you have a passion and fire, you can go for it. The challenging part is taking it from small-scale to large-scale.

Wake-up call

My journey has had many highs and lows. It was so exciting for Dirty Lamb to get into a retail store, but I wasn't expecting it to be so hard. If I knew how hard it was, I don't know if I would have started, but I'm glad I did. It was so overwhelming at first. I felt like no one understood, and it's a very lonely process. Although I work with others, it's totally different from going to a job and having coworkers. I'm going through new challenges on my own, and a lot of money is going into the products. So if I lose out on the products, it's a big deal.

One of my biggest wake-up calls happened while working with FabFitFun. Everything is very short notice in this industry, but I always want to take it on and say I can do it. One month, I had 30,000 units to get done in a three-week period. As a small business, Dirty Lamb doesn't have tons of employees, so I was doing all the work myself. I was being reckless because there were so many units and I didn't know how to handle it. I ended up not paying enough attention to the quality-control seals on a mask and was told they couldn't be accepted because half of the products weren't fully sealed. It was a huge order, and half of my revenue for that month got taken back.

Knowing what you want to do is a blessing, and you should follow your intuition on it. Use your time wisely—take your weekends or nights off and work on your passions.

IT WAS SO OVERWHELMING AT FIRST. I FELT LIKE NO ONE UNDERSTOOD, AND IT'S A VERY LONELY PROCESS.

I needed that wake-up call to realize that this is my business, not anyone else's. I picked up and moved on from that mistake very fast; I didn't harp on it at all. I knew I needed to keep moving with the mindset that the next month would be better and that crying about it wouldn't help.

My brother recently told me, "You're the CEO of Dirty Lamb, but when you come to the office, think of yourself as an employee and get to work." It was so helpful to think of it that way because sometimes I get in the mindset that I can sit back and relax since I don't have to work normal nine-to-five hours. In reality, it's constant work.

Knowing what you want to do is a blessing

I sacrificed a very comfortable job—which was also my dream job—as a NICU nurse and a steady paycheck every two weeks. I used to think I sacrificed getting married and having kids at a young age because I really wanted that. Now, it feels like less of a sacrifice and more of a blessing. I still want those things when the time is right. I decided to prioritize my business for good reasons. It's not that you can't have a relationship as an entrepreneur, but when you focus your everything on the business, it's hard to put another person first.

My best advice would be to be complete on your own. This allows you to move freely and take risks you would never be able to take if you were dependent on someone else. I'd also say start now. It's never too late, and you don't need a lot of money, but don't quit your job right away. Knowing what you want to do is a blessing, and you should follow your intuition on it. Use your time wisely—take your weekends or nights off and work on your passions.

What is "success"?

Success means providing value to others. If I weren't helping somebody else, I wouldn't feel like what I'm doing was important.

I'm most proud of being able to treat very difficult skin conditions such as cystic and hormonal acne with natural, plant-based ingredients. It's amazing to know that Dirty Lamb has been able to make both women and men feel more comfortable with themselves.

Why Cleveland?

My family is a really big reason I'm here. They're my motivation and my happiness. My dad is an immigrant from Palestine, and he's shown me that you can be given absolutely nothing and still make a name for yourself.

Our manufacturing and fulfillment center is in Akron, so having my office out of there means I can be a part of every process, which is important to me for ensuring quality control. I'm very thankful that I'm from Ohio because it's grounded me and helped make me the person I am.

SAM FLOWERS & BRITTANY BENTON

Musicians, entrepreneurs, educators, and cultural advocates

Emcee Sam Flowers, also known as Playne Jayne, delivers impactful lyrics with a dynamic stage presence and infectious energy. She also empowers youth with the tools to create and record music through her position as a program director for Notes for Notes inside the Boys & Girls Club.

Brittany Benton, also known as DJ Red-I, is a DJ, beatmaker, and owner of Brittany's Record Shop in Slavic Village. By working relentlessly as a cultural and community advocate, she has created opportunities and spaces for people to learn, collaborate, and thrive.

Together, they make up the hip-hop duo FreshProduce; own their own record label, Fresh By Nature; and are a driving force behind Fresh Fest, a family-friendly event offering music, food, art, and educational workshops in the Kinsman neighborhood.

The beginning

Sam:
Growing up, I wanted to be a version of what I am now. I own a record label with Brittany, we do FreshProduce, and I teach youth programming around hip-hop and music in general. So I'm always surrounded by music and am doing something I love 24/7.

Brittany:
I'd say something similar. I was always fascinated with music as a child. Now I sell music, I make it, I sample it, I produce it, I share it. There was one point when I wanted to be a chef because I was a kid when the food channels came out. Or, I thought I wanted to be a doctor, but then we started dissecting things in school, and I thought if I can't even cut open a frog, I can't practice medicine. But music was always there. It was one thing that would always affect my mood, and I thought it had secret powers. I wanted to learn how to harness that and use it for good.

Sam:
I used to bump Mary J. Blige's *What's the 411?* Remix album when I was a little, little kid. And then she came out with *My Life*, and I made everybody dance to the whole album at my birthday party—it was my shit. Listening to *My Life*, I realized what emotion was. I didn't know what she was talking about because I was like, "This is adult stuff." But I felt it when I listened to that album. I would learn the songs, practice them, and make my family watch me perform.

Then I got into plays, and when I was in high school I started a band called LMNTL with my brother. Our parents started believing in us, so they made us practice every day after school. We'd walk home, eat some oatmeal, then go practice. On my fifteenth birthday, I opened up for Sean Paul, so it really validated all the work I had been putting in because we beat an adult in a competition to be the opener for his show.

Meeting

Brittany:
I had met Sam before at a show and thought she was really good. It was LMNTL performing at Now That's Class. I'm not going to lie— when you hear "local band" or "local act," you support it because it's local, but you pretty much think it's going to suck. But when

Sam performed, she was the complete package. Lyrics, stage presence, energy—you don't really see that from a lot of women. Somebody might have great lyrics but they're really standoffish and weird onstage, or they have great stage presence but their content is trash.

Over the next one or two years, we kept bumping into each other. Then at another show I reached out to her. We both have backgrounds in education, so it was very cool to get together and organize for the sake of young people and community since that's always been a part of what we did anyway. We've benefited from older people helping us, cultivating us, and reaching out to us. At the same time, we also know what it's like to suffer at the hands of older predatory people who see your potential, and if they can't crush it or steal it, they want to subdue it, misdirect it, or exploit it negatively.

Sam:
Brittany had beats, I had raps, and then it just developed into a record label, a tour, youth programs, a festival. We had weekly meetings where we were working on music and learning how to set up an independent record label. Literally we got on Google, watched some stuff, wrote some notes, and just did it. I was excited, but I was also mad that I had been doing music this long and didn't understand how easy it could be to just take a few more hours and actually own what I was making. It's not as intimidating as I thought it'd be. A few months in, Brittany was talking about how the sound is organic and it's not fast food. She said "fresh produce" and I was like, "Wait, stop, that's it." That's how we got our name.

Within that year of having our own business entity for the music, people started approaching us differently and offering us different opportunities than when we were musicians.

Brittany:
The original Fresh By Nature, which is now the name of our record label, was me selling shea butter, incense, soaps, and imports. When we wanted to start a label, we released stuff out of that entity because I already owned the business. Musically, we wanted to represent something fresh and different, so we kept the name. Within that year of having our own business entity for the music, people started approaching us differently and offering us different opportunities than when we were musicians.

This is what the record industry is built on—exploiting black people. That shit stops in 2020.

Exploitation in the music industry

Sam:
There are people I've dealt with in my life since I was thirteen who took me under their wing and helped me grow, but then once I grew, they tried to cut my head off. Which is sad. And it's a story you hear a lot in music.

Brittany:
In terms of black people in this country, especially black people in arts, it's been habitually made for us to be an exploited class. We have so much raw, natural passion, energy, talent, and insight. We're the most innovative group in the country because our situation has forced us to be. But music history in America is just generations of how black people are exploited and cheated out of their money, rights, and royalties. Every genre—from ragtop to blues, rock to country, hip-hop to R&B to house—starts in the black country or the black streets and is considered obscure and weird. By the time it can be commodified and copied, it's whitewashed and in somebody else's hands, and the originators are still left dejected, poor, and unrecognized. When does this stop?

Sam:
This is what the record industry is built on—exploiting black people. That shit stops in 2020. Own your own label, own your own business. I'm working with kids whom I hope to lead in a positive way in the future. I'm building my knowledge so I can help them learn how to build a label. I've got a kid who just dropped a mixtape. We're about to invest in his record label right now.

Brittany:
We're sick of seeing people being used as artistic sharecroppers. We see how the music industry is for our people and how integral we've been to it from the beginning, yet we're always marginalized and left on the periphery. There's always going to be a new generation with fresh exploitation, and that's why people are constantly getting discarded. And that's why you'll see the *Behind the Music VH1* episodes about how people fall from grace because it's nothing but sharks and people looking to exploit.

Sam:
And then it turns whitewashed and they cash out.

Brittany:
And they call it pop music.

Creating music and Fresh Fest

Brittany:
To make music, you have to have a level of comfort with being emotional and exposed. We've been blessed to have so much music that's connected with us and has transported us just through our headphones that I feel like if I don't say something, then there's a little black girl or black boy somewhere who won't get the message in the bottle. People respect and embrace someone like Lauryn Hill who's out there with dreadlocks, dark skin, unapologetic, saying, "You don't have to look exactly like me to connect with me." It's like, damn, what would it look like if two sisters like me and Sam are onstage not trying to be something we're not? That speaks to people.

In media, we're told that unless you're a punch line or some kind of overexaggerated character, you can't be dark-skinned or fat. Missy Elliot, for example, back in the day was like, "Yeah, that's what they say, but fuck that," and it was like an exhale for everybody. When I was looking for people I could identify and connect with, or I was

SUCCESS IS LEGACY BUILDING.

catching hell in school for being the only black kid in Brecksville, or I had to hide my culture or the way I speak, I put headphones on. It transported me to a bunch of people just like me. They were feeding me things that I wouldn't have been able to get anywhere else. It came to me like a message in a bottle, so who are we to not do that for the next generation? Music saved my life. It pushed my desire to understand knowledge of self.

Sam:
Missy Elliot, Mary J. Blige, and Lil' Kim are like my mothers in music. And shout out to Freddie Mercury. And James Brown. And Tina Turner.

Fresh Fest Cleveland is a product of our two years working with the FreshLo (fresh, local, and equitable) Garden Valley initiative. We were given a grant to placemake inside the Garden Valley neighborhood. We were the hip-hop leg of a summer program that taught youth gardening, culinary skills, entrepreneurship, and music. We created an open mic at WOVU out of this program. Kids started a juice business from the gardening program at Ridd-All farm. Our youth got to perform in a festival in their own community. The festival had music, education, and fresh food and is really a cool combination of what we did and cultivated in these last two years through our work in the community.

Being community-minded is going to help you exponentially. We can really see the effects of what we're doing in the neighborhood when youth get our message in a bottle through the music. A six-figure salary can't match that.

Brittany:
With Fresh Fest, we gave people a music festival comparable to the bigger names in our neighborhood, which newspapers called a slum. It was a safe space in a place that so many people had moved out of, stayed away from, or said, "Don't you ever go there." People from community development corporations from more affluent neighborhoods even came down to see what was going on.

Community leadership

Sam:
Right now I'm the Cleveland program director for Notes for Notes, a national organization. I teach and develop kids and organize different workshops and instructional sessions for them. They ask me

to help them work on a song or learn to play an instrument, and I walk them through that individually or as a group. I also started Sam Supreme, which is my solo adventure under my label Art, Money, Merch.

Brittany:
I own Brittany's Record Shop, and we have a beatmaker's night called Beat Freak, which is going into its third year. Every month, we have different producers play their sets showcasing original music. Usually when you go to an open mic night, it's all about the singer and the poet, but we wanted to do it in reverse by putting the beatmaker first. Hearing things over loudspeakers can be part of the finishing process because sometimes you're making stuff in your headphones or in your bedroom all day. It's built a vibe and a family of people who make beats. Most of the people who attend

are emcees, and there have been a couple of projects that have happened because vocalists connected with producers at these events.

Whenever you want to create a scene, it's not enough just to have creative people in the room because that's very touch-and-go. You have to have the creativity, the content, some kind of economy or circulation, and a designated space. In documentaries, there's always a group of bars or concert halls or maybe somebody's mom's basement that was essential to the growth of the scene. People have to have a place to go to make these things happen, whether it's music, art, or politics.

Making it to the next level

Sam:
A challenge is staying on top of the visions that we have and making them actually happen in the real world.

Brittany:
One thing we always have to make sure we do is take an inventory of the people around us. Once you're committed to whatever your work is, there are people on the inside trying to tear you down. It's like a video game. You made it to the next level, but in the end you're still going to have to face that final challenge or that final opponent.

We've sacrificed relationships. When you're walking in your light and moving in your purpose, things become black and white. All those people who were messing around in a gray area have to pick a side. I feel like the relationships that did fall away were people who only wanted to see us succeed until we were doing better than them. When things started taking off, my boyfriend turned into an ex. I sacrificed a corporate job that was really good in the sense that I was on pace to make six figures. But once my supervisor found out I was opening another record store and that I just came off of a tour before I started working there, they gave me an ultimatum. They were literally asking me to decide whether to pursue my life's purpose versus a job. With certain jobs, if you have a life outside of it and you're not a complete drone for their cause, then you're going to feel a lot of resistance.

What is "success"?

Sam:
Success is legacy building.

Brittany:
Your success is the people who come after you. If there are ten more FreshProduces that come out of Cleveland, that's success because we ensured that. Being community-minded is going to help you exponentially. We can really see the effects of what we're doing in the neighborhood when youth get our message in a bottle through the music. A six-figure salary can't match that. At the end of the day, I just want to see our community in a better position than I found it.

An ideal picture of Cleveland

Brittany:
Cleveland has a huge equity issue. I feel like it's the most segregated major city in the country. There are things that can be improved in terms of standard of living, education, and health. We've got so many renowned colleges and one of the best hospital systems, but we're still one of the unhealthiest cities.

Sam:
Number one in infant mortality.

Brittany:
Cleveland has been a model for modern urbanization, which includes segregation, white flight, and tearing apart communities just to further expand outside. A lot of the things that you see in terms of suffering and poverty, especially among the black community, are a result of that. Cleveland is still a technically black-majority city, but our voice—our legitimate voice of the people, not just token figureheads and politicians—is very much unheard. The streets are bleeding, the children are crying. Everybody's talking about a corporate solution or an injection or outside investment and all these other big words, but what about the people who are here?

Sam:
We're getting a lot of development projects all over the city, but it's not being reflected in the people who've been here for years. They've been kicked out. Shit's gotta change. It can change because we're getting a lot of resources—it's just not being reflected in everyday people.

THIS IS OUR HOME. YOU DON'T LIKE IT? CHANGE IT.

Brittany:
Cleveland will never, ever, ever be a success until it works diligently to undo the wrongs it did, especially to the black population. We get a lot of surface-level shine and recognition for our work in the community, but the city's supposed to be doing these things. Why are we having to build Fresh Fest in a place that's considered a food desert when the city can literally just put up a market?

Sam:
They don't take the time to get to know the people and their struggles so they can actually put resources in a place where they can help. They don't really care about helping people—they just want a picture in *The Plain Dealer* saying they spent the check on something that looks nice.

Brittany:
We're black people in America. Our idea of success and longevity counters the American vision. America has designated us as an underclass to struggle and not succeed and just be a source of extraction for constant generations of incoming people. Unless it works diligently on these issues, Cleveland will be another place that's corny, soulless, and gentrified, built on the bones of the black underclass so everybody can have their lattes and GMO-free, fair-trade bullshit when ten years ago it was a project. But none of the people who lived in the projects were able to grow and flourish with the city, and they're living on the outskirts somewhere. We fight and do what we can to try and create a safe space for us to flourish, and sometimes if we can't thrive, we're just trying to create a space for our people to survive.

Sam:
And just be.

But Cleveland is home. It's unique. I feel like I've been a part of the Cleveland scene since I was thirteen years old. This place is what built me and prepared me for the world. Without Cleveland's people, bars, scenes, and everything about the city, I wouldn't be who I am.

Brittany:
It's definitely home. People always complain that there's not a lot going on here, it moves too slow, or it's not as cultivated as it could be. But if I were to be a DJ in L.A., I'd be competing with twenty people just like me in my age group. And mind you, I'd have to pay L.A.'s cost of living. The resources needed to have a record

store and do this stuff in New York would probably be tenfold. In Cleveland, if you dedicate yourself, you can be at the top of your field locally, and then it's a lot easier to get opportunities in L.A. or in London or New York.

This is our home. You don't like it? Change it. Make the bed, wash and change the drapes, mop the floor, clean that shit up. It takes people and processes and resources to turn things around.

KATHY BLACKMAN

Founder and owner of Grog Shop and B-Side Lounge

As the owner of the iconic music venue the Grog Shop and its downstairs counterpart, the B-Side Lounge, Kathy Blackman attracts national acts to perform and showcases local talent on her intimate stage in Coventry. She has hustled to build her business into the local treasure that it is by doing everything from bartending to managing a team to dealing with the occasional mosh pit.

Kathy at the Grog Shop in Coventry
Photo by Ryan Gerard

The beginning

I don't think I had any dreams like growing up to be a ballerina. Maybe I did at one point. I do remember pretending I was going to be a belly dancer or something, but I might have been like four years old. So no, I did not really have any grand goals.

Getting here was sort of a fluke. I just fell into it. I liked music, I liked bands, I liked going out. But I didn't graduate from college and decide that I wanted to own a bar and promote bands. While I was writing for a local newspaper and waitressing in University Circle, a couple of guys I was working with said, "We should open a bar," and we just sort of went for it with very little knowledge except that we were all in the restaurant business. I didn't really know what I wanted to do career-wise at that point; I thought I'd just try it for a short period of time and see what happened.

It was exciting in the beginning—I was involved 24/7 at the bar for the first few years. I did everything. I was probably bartending five nights a week. It was also my social life and my identity for a long time.

Evolving

Within a couple of years, both of my partners were gone and it was just me. What started as booking a few bands here and there became national acts, then hosting shows seven nights a week. Gradually over the first few years, it evolved into more of a music club than just a corner bar, and here I am twenty-five years later. I have no idea how. Or why.

As my life went on and I got married and had kids, my priorities shifted a bit. The Grog Shop is still my first child, but clearly I love my real children more. I own the B-Side downstairs too, but it's kind of like my redheaded stepchild. I used to feel like I had babies to take care of at home, then had to come here and babysit different kinds of children.

It evolved into more of a music club than just a corner bar, and here I am twenty-five years later. I have no idea how. Or why.

Especially in the last ten years, I'm definitely less hands-on as far as being here at night, being here for the shows, and dealing with customers. I'll still be here at night if we're really busy, if a band I love is playing, or if we're short-staffed. I'll still jump behind the bar, mop floors, or load in the band's equipment if need be. But I rely much more on my staff now because I have chosen to take a step back.

A roller-coaster of challenges

A misconception about running the Grog Shop is that it's easy and glamorous—which I do not believe is true in any way, shape, or form. It seems like a happy, party atmosphere, but it is not. It is work, and it is *tough*. People will walk in and see a packed bar and think you're making so much money, but they don't see you on a Tuesday night when there are twelve people in here and I have to pay the band $1,000.

Financial strain in a business like this is always a factor. We're a shoestring operation and don't have that much to fall back on if things aren't going right. As great as one week may be, the next week your air conditioner breaks and your cooler breaks and you get hit with some back taxes, or a show cancels. Shit like that happens all the time. It's very much a roller-coaster, so you have to be able to deal with things without getting too flustered. You need to have a very thick skin in this business. There's a lot that can go wrong, and you just have to know that you're going to wake up tomorrow and it'll be another day. I try to be pretty laid-back about all the uncertainty.

During the time when I was spending every minute here, it's what I wanted to do. So I don't think I've sacrificed very much. Once I had kids, I decided to change my lifestyle, but I'd already lived and experienced thirteen years of being at the bar every day. It was time to transition. Maybe I've sacrificed privacy a little bit. Cleveland is a very small town, so anywhere you go you're going to see people you know. I don't really mind this, but it's not for everybody to be such a public person. Through this work I've gained a sense of accomplishment. And a lot of freedom. If I want to go on vacation for two weeks, I can. There may be a price to pay, but I certainly feel I can do what I want, when I want.

Music is important

There's a lot that Cleveland has to offer, but I think the music scene is just as important as our cultural attractions and sports teams.

Photo by Ryan Gerard

PEOPLE WILL WALK IN AND SEE A PACKED BAR AND THINK YOU'RE MAKING SO MUCH MONEY, BUT THEY DON'T SEE YOU ON A TUESDAY NIGHT WHEN THERE ARE TWELVE PEOPLE IN HERE AND I HAVE TO PAY THE BAND $1,000.

Music is a social and creative outlet for people. Especially in this day and age when there's very little interpersonal connection because people are on their phones so much, seeing a band is real experience. You're connecting with other people *in person*, not staring at a screen. It's also good for the community as a whole to have a scene where people can be supportive of each other.

It makes me feel really good to receive acknowledgment from bands that feel like the Grog was a part of their education. Occasionally I'll go to a throwback show—like some punk band that hasn't played here in years—and they'll tell me how glad they are that we're still here. They'll say that they started their careers here and it's places like this that keep them going.

I think the music scene is just as important as our cultural attractions and sports teams. Music is a social and creative outlet for people. Especially in this day and age when there's very little interpersonal connection because people are on their phones so much, seeing a band is real experience.

An ideal picture of Cleveland

Cleveland would be safer in general. And we'd have more sunny days. The city itself is changing so much that there are pockets that are doing great and I feel like Coventry has been left behind a little. I'd love to see more businesses start up here and be able to make it.

STEPHANIE SHELDON

Founder and creative CEO of Cleveland Flea; life and business coach

Stephanie Sheldon is an entrepreneur and business coach on a mission to Defend Creativity™. As the founder of Cleveland Flea, she built a creative economy that fosters the founding and growth of hundreds of new small businesses. Her relentless optimism and grand vision of how things could be have left an indelible mark on Cleveland.

The beginning

When I was a kid, I wanted to be something creative. I loved baking, building, and designing. I've had a side hustle my entire life that always went a little bit beyond hobby status, and I always cared about doing things really well. For my graduation, I made seven Martha Stewart cakes just because I was really interested in learning how to do it well. I always thought if I could do things well, other people might value them. Even though I didn't understand that was business, I was working that way.

I went to architecture school and had quite a few creative jobs while attending. Then I started getting interested in entrepreneurship, moved to Cleveland, and realized I didn't know many creative people here. I started digging around and found that there were creative people here, but none of them were really doing anything publicly. They were all hobby status and very hard to find. I started bringing them together at dinners and networking events, trying to understand and uncover the creative community living in Cleveland. I quickly realized that most people would love to do their passion projects full-time but felt they didn't know how and didn't have enough money. I thought, *Well, I'll just solve that for you.*

Founding the Flea

The architecture firm I was working at closed, and I found myself out of a job. I worked at two restaurants and had a lot of extra time to think and get inspired. I started studying the handmade world from a business perspective and also started my own handmade business doing stationery design, graphic design, and branding. Finding my way wasn't clear-cut or quick. But I started allowing myself to see what my heart was into, and that led me toward helping handmade businesses solve their financial problems. They weren't able to move forward or make money because they didn't have access to each other or an audience.

Through studying handmade businesses, I realized there were a few events happening that supported creative small businesses, but none were happening more than once or twice a year, which is not often enough to grow a robust creative economy. Plus, a lot of makers weren't yet established enough to get into those events or weren't the right fit for the audience. I knew there was an opportunity to support the small business community in a new way. Thus, Cleveland Flea was born! Cleveland Flea started as a monthly market during warm months. For six years, it was like a business incubator because showing up every month allowed vendors to build business skills and get better quickly.

It solves a financial problem and a business problem for most creatives, which is why hundreds of businesses have been built because of Cleveland Flea that would not exist otherwise.

Taking the leap into starting my own business was really torturous, to be honest. My business was a creative pioneer in Cleveland. For the most part, I had to create everything myself; I couldn't look to other people for how they did things. I've been running a market for seven years now. People from around the country ask me how I can help them either start a market in their city or improve existing markets, so I'm getting more into business coaching and consulting. Markets are the bedrock of a small business economy, and we can learn a lot of lessons from all the ways they're taking shape. Three years ago I became a life coach, so I'm working with business owners on overcoming emotional and business challenges and maintaining creative health.

High expectations

Our mission is first and foremost to help Cleveland love itself more. We have that mission because Cleveland has massive city pride, but it sometimes gets down on itself in ways I found curious, being an outsider. From my perspective, I only see possibility and growth. The Flea enables hundreds of business owners to make money doing what they love for people they love. Even people who just visit might look at them and think, *Maybe one day I could do that, too.*

It solves a financial problem and a business problem for most creatives, which is why hundreds of businesses have been built because of Cleveland Flea that would not exist otherwise. It only takes a few shoppers getting excited about a business for the owner to truly believe in their dreams, and we have more than a few shoppers giving encouragement to business owners here. It's

TO ME, SUCCESS IS EVOLUTION. IT'S DECIDING WHO YOU WANT TO BE AND THEN BECOMING IT AND GOING THROUGH THE STRUGGLE TO GET THERE.

magical. It's really because Cleveland is such a special place that this works.

There's a larger stability in the creative independent economy because of us. Our event is always geared toward delivering a minimum of five thousand shoppers, which requires a huge marketing effort. If I couldn't deliver shoppers to my vendors, the entire cycle wouldn't work. That took a huge amount of sacrifice, cost me hundreds of thousands of marketing dollars, and delayed my ability to make money for my business for many years because I would put every dollar back into that mission. I knew stabilizing the creative economy was more important than me earning a big paycheck. I've sacrificed a lot—energy, time, money, sanity, mental health, stability.

In the United States, we don't know how to support, care for, and interact with independent small-business owners. The rise in cancel culture, call-out culture, and Amazon-style expectations is unfair and unhealthy to small-business owners. The Amazon model is to get it as fast as possible at the cheapest price. This really undoes an independent economy because we don't get that scale. We're human beings. Small businesses don't have access to tax breaks. Independent small-business owners are the least supported, yet we have the highest expectations because you can identify a person when they own a small business. You can't complain to a specific person at Amazon, whereas when you're in a personal relationship with a small-business owner, you can transfer your anger to one person.

What I've gained is a deep understanding of people and business. I really feel like I understand what it means to be a human doing creative things. I know our value in the community—that's really important. I have a ton of confidence in myself because I've stayed committed for this long, even though it's been hard.

What is "success"?

To me, success is evolution. It's deciding who you want to be and then becoming it and going through the struggle to get there. It's not the end result—it's the going through it.

I'm really proud that we've stayed committed and have allowed ourselves to be in the struggle and remain true to our original belief system. I'm really proud of our large-scale, long-term effect. I'm really proud of shoppers who are part of our creative community

and who continue to show up and support these businesses with positivity and love. I think it's all very interconnected. We could have had a marketplace that was devoid of that energy, but I set it up at the very beginning to harness that.

Creative thinking will solve all of our crises.

We created the trademark Defend Creativity™ this year for Cleveland Flea. Creativity gets put in this bucket of what it produces—things like paintings and art—but it's also a way of thinking about the world. My calling in life is to make people understand that creativity is not just the visuals you see—it's also an expression of how you care about the world, which can be expressed in so many ways. Creative thinking will solve all of our crises. That's how any evolution happens: people think differently.

An ideal picture of Cleveland

Cleveland is extremely segregated. Our city government could be improved to respond to that and have more of a visionary approach to what the next ten years will look like here. There's too much poverty, too much illiteracy, and schools aren't funded well enough. These are problems that happen all over—it's not just a Cleveland problem—but the city has to be more creative in response to that. We need more people with diverse ideas who have access to capital and are bringing their unique viewpoints to developing our city.

Why Cleveland?

I'm in Cleveland because we needed each other. I needed something to love really deeply, and Cleveland needed somebody to love it very deeply and stay committed to it. Context matters—I couldn't do this anywhere. The right type of atmosphere with the right type of people with the right type of city pride was necessary for it to be possible. The Flea literally needs a community exactly like Cleveland to be successful. I would have to study an entirely different set of variables to make it work in another city. Cleveland is full of so much opportunity and possibility. It's a really exceptional place to live. If we can enable people to connect to their purpose, we'll continue to be able to keep creatives here.

Best piece of advice

Choose something you're obsessed with—that you love so much. Have high commitment to it. Have courage during that process. Be willing to endure discomfort in order to grow. Find a community. Perfection is impossible; don't work toward perfection. Find other people who believe in a grand vision of things. Fill your world with the words of really big thinkers and people who are doing great things. Let them be your teachers. Allow yourself to be changed, even when it's really hard. The best thing that's ever happened to me was going to life coaching school; I learned something fundamental, which is that my thoughts are optional. I can have whatever thoughts about myself I want, so I decided to let go of a lot of the negative ones and pick new ones. That changed everything for me.

A lot of us are scared to get outside our bubble. We avoid change and challenge by only getting to know people in our comfort zone because it's easier to navigate socially. But when you get to know people who are different from you, who have opposing viewpoints or have lived a very different life, you get a richer life. A bigger life.

JASMYN CARTER

Entertainer

In her comedy sketches, Jasmyn Carter expertly switches back and forth between characters. Whether she's impersonating a cranky grandma, a ladies' man, or a classic millennial, the result is both hilarious and painfully relatable—two turnkey elements for good comedy. She's earned countless laughs on stages across the country as well as from the 125K+ followers on her social media channels. In 2016, she became the first woman and the youngest person to win the Cleveland Comedy Festival.

Jasmyn in Bedford

The beginning

Growing up, I wanted to be a bunch of things. At first I wanted to be an Olympic track star, and then my dad said they take steroids. So that dream was gone. Then it was like little-kid dreams—veterinarian, teacher, open a daycare. Then I thought I wanted to be an athletic trainer or nutritionist. I didn't know I was funny until people told me. I just thought I was me. I think I realized that I wanted to do something in entertainment after I saw Kevin Hart and Beyoncé perform live. I was like, "This is where I belong."

I started out by making videos on Vine and Facebook, but I didn't start doing stand-up until 2015. The first time I got onstage was after a bad breakup. I was like, you know what, forget him—I'm going to be famous. So I went to do stand-up at EuroGyro. It's not even a dive bar—it's like a dive restaurant in Kent. I got there two hours early. I was drinking mango Three Olives in a water bottle because I had to get my mind right. I don't even remember what I talked about. But at that moment, I knew I wanted to do stand-up and entertainment for the rest of my life, and I haven't stopped since. My first mentor told me to say yes to as many things as possible. So I did, and I still say yes to everything. I've done shows outside, in houses, at churches with children and babies, and in front of nobody.

Just do it

For anyone aspiring to have a career in comedy, I say just do it. I know that's cliché, but just do it. If you think it's funny, say it. You'll never know what's going to work until you try. What works for one person won't work for the next person. And if six months later you think, *What was I thinking?* so what? It's like riding a bike. No one gives you a sheet of paper and is like, "This is how you ride the bike." That doesn't mean you don't know how to do it. My favorite quote is from Will Smith: "The first step is you have to say you can." I even got it tattooed. If you don't think you can do something, you won't be able to. The mind is very powerful. People trick themselves into dying every day.

Whoever works the hardest is going to achieve the most. At the end of the day, we all want to be seen and heard, but it's not about the talent. It's about who's going to put in the work. If you're not doing the work, someone else is. When you're asleep, someone's up. When you're up, someone else is asleep.

Most of my day is spent writing—I'm probably writing for 70 percent of the day. My brain is constantly working; I can't escape myself. So when it's time to go to bed, that's when my brain decides to write the best jokes ever and keep me up for the next five hours. Then I finally go to sleep from exhaustion, only to wake up and realize that those thoughts were very dumb and I was up for no reason. But I have to write it down or it will bother me. I talk about everything except for politics. Politics is one of those things that instantly divides the room. I don't want to divide the room and then try to bring them back on my side. It's not that I don't care about what's going on—it's just not what I'm there for.

> *It's like riding a bike. No one gives you a sheet of paper and is like, "This is how you ride the bike." That doesn't mean you don't know how to do it.*

My journey has been ups and down, but good. Good as in it's been a fun, growing experience because I started when I was twenty. As I'm growing, my jokes are growing with me. Not many people get to do that; many people start doing comedy as adults, but here I am still getting to know myself. Sometimes the nerves don't go away. Sometimes I still feel like a little girl standing in church trying to give an Easter speech. But most of the time I feel good. I'm in my element. I'm happy. That's not the only time I feel happy, but it's when I feel it the most.

Overcoming sacrifices, challenges, and discrimination

I've made a lot of sacrifices. Time. Money. Relationships. Friendships. Energy. A secure lifestyle. I was in college. I graduated at the top of my high school class, so school was my thing. I was supposed to be the one to make a lot of money—the lawyer, the doctor, THAT. But that wasn't working for me. So yeah, I sacrificed everything. Literally love, relationships, friendships, family, everything.

Sometimes people don't get it; they don't understand what it takes. They don't understand why I can't come to Grandma's fiftieth

ANYTIME YOU DO SOMETHING FOR FAME OR MONEY, IT'S NOT GOING TO TURN OUT WELL.

birthday party and do a mic for two minutes, get paid $5 to do it, and pay $60 in gas just to get there. They say, "You're not you." But I am me. I'm just evolving. I'm stepping into my true self—they just don't get it. If it's your birthday or wedding and I have a show, I'm not coming. I'm not going to miss opportunities because others feel insecure. At first it was hard, but I'm numb to it now.

There have been a lot of other challenges, too, such as trying to get stage time and getting bumped off a show for someone else. You can get kicked off a show by other women because you're a woman. I've faced discrimination. Being a black woman, it happens. I know if I'm being discriminated against as soon as I hit the stage. Then I show them why their judgment is wrong. I show them that whatever they thought of me, I'm the complete opposite. Sometimes people come up to me after the show and say, "Aw man, you were great" and kind of kiss my ass a little bit. They'll be like, "You know, women aren't usually funny, but you— YOU—were great." I just turn around and walk away.

Lucille Ball changed the game for female comedians. Up until that time, women weren't funny. They weren't lead characters—they were sub characters, like "I cook, I clean." I also love Jada Smith and a couple of my peers whom I do comedy with. I admire their work ethic, talent, and intelligence. It pushes me to do better when the people around me are doing well.

Working out keeps me leveled. Because comedians are always in our heads, we need some way to escape. Some people go to a comedy show to escape, some people play music, some people drink or do drugs. I work out.

What is "success"?

To me, success is being happy in my business life and personal life. My vision for myself is to be as many things as I can be—a comedian, actor, director, producer, entertainer, and if I could sing, I would do that, too. I don't want anybody to put me in a box, because we're such advanced creatures that we can be more than one thing. Society makes us think we have to choose one thing, but we don't.

Comedy is a long career. Anytime you do something for fame or money, it's not going to turn out well. Karma is real. Do it for the love of it. Why would you want to be famous? They only reason I want to be famous is to make as many people laugh as possible.

Why Cleveland?

I'm from Cleveland. I think it's great here. It has a lot of potential that often gets cut in half because of crime and poverty. People overlook Cleveland, but it's filled with some of the most talented people in the world. It's a great stepping-stone for comedy because we have lots of different clubs here—you get the black rooms, white rooms, mixed rooms, young rooms, and old rooms. Plus, you can easily travel to New York and Chicago and other surrounding cities to develop your material even more.

An ideal picture of Cleveland

Less poverty and homelessness. People already come here all the time to shoot their movies because the taxes are low. There are abandoned houses everywhere—let's tear those down and build a production studio.

ANJUA MAXIMO

Co-owner of
GrooveRyde

Anjua Maximo inspires people through movement and builds community at her one-stop shop boutique fitness studio, GrooveRyde, which she built with her husband, Zosimo Maximo. What started with training instructors to be mini life coaches in her basement has grown into multiple locations across Cleveland. Anjua has earned group fitness instructor certifications in many formats, including pole dancing, yoga, and classical Pilates.

Anjua in her Van Aken District studio

The beginning

When I was a kid, I wanted to be a jockey who also had a fashion line and was a veterinarian. I thought I could do all these things at once. I would have this office where I would see the animals on one side, my boutique on the other side, and then I would ride horses on weekends at the races. My dreams were smashed when I was told I was already too tall to be a jockey at age ten.

I was not the kid who liked sports. It wasn't fun for me until I found ballet. I loved to dance, but even ballet felt too constrained. I was always daydreaming and never going the right direction, so I never felt like I really belonged there, either. But I knew I loved to move and I loved to dance. I went to a high school for performing arts in New York where they introduced me to different styles of movement, modern dance, Pilates, and my first taste of yoga. In college, I found movement teachers who further piqued my interest, especially around Pilates.

Finding fitness

I wanted to be healthy, but I just couldn't find the thing I loved to do in the gym. To me, if it wasn't fun, I wasn't motivated to do it. At this point, I was in L.A., married, and an actor. One day, my trainer suggested I try a pole-dancing class. I went by myself to this really dark room filled with forty other women who were just as terrified as I was. I swung around the pole once, and it was instantly a feeling of freedom, of childlike wonderment. I was buzzing after that. I continued to go back to that studio. Then I got pregnant, but the whole time throughout my pregnancy, I was waiting until I could get back to the class.

I'd always been told, "You're really skinny—you're weak—you're small." People would try to make me feel like I couldn't box or do aggressive workouts. Pole dancing was the first time that I really felt like a superhero. I was stronger in a way that I never thought I could be. Beyond that, there was this beautiful bond forming between the women. There was true support and excitement to be together. You would see them swinging their hips and feeling so powerful. It was intoxicating to watch.

I wanted to teach people to do that, so I went to a training. It was very rigorous—almost eight hours a day for two months. I got injured putting my body through an extreme training after not having worked out seriously. It was intense. I went on to teach pole for three years. It was never really about shaking your booty or performing. The intention of the class was always about doing it for yourself. If you chose to do it for other people, that was fine, but primarily it was about discovering and investigating what you really liked, what felt good to you, and what you found sexy, as opposed to what you were taught or made to believe.

The body holds emotion and trauma. When we move it in certain ways, those things will unexpectedly come up.

The creator of it all was the woman who taught me how to read bodies. I could essentially tell what someone's emotional story was by just watching them dance. Some really heavy emotional stuff was coming up for some people because the body holds emotion and trauma. When we move it in certain ways, those things will unexpectedly come up, so we literally would have students crying. The thing that was missing for me was that the teachers didn't know how to hold space for these women when they were cracking open. In my mind, I was always planting the seed that I was going to get certified in life coaching, learn more about the body and trauma, and create my own version of it.

California to Cleveland

My husband was a director in Hollywood and had been yearning to return to his background in sports. We left California and moved to Cleveland because he took a job as a content creator for *Stack* magazine, which worked with athletes. During that time, I had found my way to Lululemon. Their focus, beyond selling great yoga clothes, was developing people to be leaders in the world. Working there taught me how to set goals and create a vision for my life. They would ask questions to really get me to think, create a plan, and understand what I needed to do to get to that point. I transferred with Lululemon and became the manager of the Eton showroom before it became an actual store. Then I left for a while, had my son, came back, and ran the store for another couple of years.

I had never been to Cleveland; I literally moved here sight unseen. Within a few days of moving, I fell in love. My kids could go out and play by themselves, which was a whole new feeling because I had grown up in Manhattan as the girl in the tower on the eighteenth floor. The kids in the neighborhood didn't even know I existed until I was old enough to go downstairs because my mother had kept me safely away from the street. To have the complete opposite just blew my mind. The people were really nice—somebody actually baked me a pie! Everybody wanted to embrace us, whether we liked it or not. I fell in love with that. Cleveland had everything I wanted—music, food, art, the cool kids, and a little bit of funk.

Dusting off a dream

Right about the same moment, my husband and I were both feeling like we were hitting walls in our careers. I had gotten away from my dream of opening a studio because I was so involved with Lululemon. So I revisited my goals. When I pulled them back out and dusted them off, the studio idea came back. We ran with the idea that GrooveRyde would be a boutique studio experience,

meaning that it's smaller, there's an intimate feel, there's more connection between teacher and guest, and we put our own twist on everything. We also knew that we wanted our teachers to be superinspirational, like mini life coaches. Guests need that because they're coming in with fear and already thinking they can't do it, along with the negativity of their whole day. We would be the one-stop shop. And that's pretty much how GrooveRyde came to be. We wanted to create extraordinary experiences that elevated people from the inside out.

Taking the leap into entrepreneurship, a lot of people thought I was crazy because my husband and I were older and had two young kids. But I felt that Lululemon had actually been great preparation for running my own business because I was trained to run their store like it was my own. I took all of that knowledge, and Zosimo brought his background in television. Everything we knew we rolled into this and didn't really doubt that we could do it. Obviously, we knew it would be hard, but we didn't know what *kind* of hard it would be. Working nine-to-five was difficult as well. It's challenging but it's ours, which makes it feel like less of a burden.

I've sacrificed a little peace of mind because it is precarious to know that you don't have a net underneath you... But I think it would have been a greater sacrifice of self to remain in roles that didn't really fulfill us.

In the beginning, construction was running behind. The first space was supposed to open in November, and we actually didn't open until the following summer. Yet we bought all the bikes and had already been training instructors in the basement of our house. Before a Lululemon would open, they'd have a showroom to test the community and see what the response was. I thought we could to do the same thing. So we rented a U-Haul and started bringing our bikes to collaborate with other studios that didn't have bikes or other things that we offered. We'd have some people show up who were introduced to their studio, and their members were introduced to our budding concept, and that's how the word started to get out. We had a reputation before we had an actual studio. It was kind of a crazy idea, but it worked.

Finding a groove

When we finally did open the Woodmere space, that's when it got real as far as the challenges. Classes didn't fill up immediately, so we were constantly reminding the instructors that if you teach one person, you teach as if there are twenty people in the room. Very quickly came the developers—that's when the second studio opened downtown, followed by Van Aken. We later closed the downtown studio. That I attribute to moving too quickly and not doing enough investigation. We opened three studios in about three years.

In my experience, one of the biggest challenges is working with a spouse. Some days they get on your nerves, some days it's great, some days you clash in your styles. On those days when you just can't wait to get out of work, go home, relax, have a glass of wine, and maybe tell your person about it, you open the door and they're there again. What we have learned is to allow each other space to grow in the areas we're good at and not micromanage each other. It also has been a huge challenge for us to learn how to create boundaries about when to talk about work and when not to. We're both creative, so we love to share ideas. That's fun for us, but at the same time it's still work, so when do we shut that off? We're working on creating that space at home so the kids see us working and aren't terrified of entrepreneurship because Mom and Dad look really stressed all the time. We want them to be inspired by it—to see how hard we're working and how we get through the tough moments.

I've sacrificed sleep—a lot of it. It's really hard to turn our brains off at the end of the night. I've sacrificed a little peace of mind because it's precarious to know that you don't have a net underneath you. But then I remind myself that nothing is secure. Companies close, layoffs happen. I think it would have been a greater sacrifice of self to remain in roles that didn't really fulfill us. I've gained even more clarity about my purpose. It's allowed me more time with my kids. I work a hundred hours a week, but I decide which hours those are. I really, really love that freedom.

What is "success"?

Success is when I see this place full of smiling faces. That does not necessarily translate into dollars yet, so right now I'm measuring our success by the response of the guests who are here, the feedback we're getting, and the fact that they keep coming back.

As an entrepreneur, my best advice is to study, study, study. Study all the successful places that are doing what you're doing, and study all the places that failed.

Why Cleveland?

Cleveland is very supportive of local entrepreneurship and growing the city. New York and L.A. are always growing, constantly building, and it's not very special to them when someone opens a business. Here, when someone opens a business, it's a celebration. I was really happy to find that we have so many resources to support us, like Jumpstart, that were willing to give their knowledge for free.

I think we could have done this in New York or L.A., but it would have been even harder because there are a lot of boutique fitness concepts in those cities. What they may be missing is the humanity piece because there isn't any community. The Midwest

FITNESS, MUSIC, FUN, AN INFECTIOUS ENERGY—ALL THOSE THINGS SERVE TO BRING PEOPLE TOGETHER. HOPEFULLY THAT TRICKLES OUT INTO THE WORLD.

vibe is definitely something that makes GrooveRyde special. Fitness, music, fun, an infectious energy—all those things serve to bring people together. Hopefully that trickles out into the world.

An ideal version of Cleveland

I would love to see more integration. That was a concern of mine when I moved here, coming from New York City, where it's such a melting pot. How are they going to react to my children, who are mixed Filipino, black, and Chinese? I would love to see downtown flourish, but I don't think the city does enough for incentivizing entrepreneurs to create the amenities that people moving down there need.

ERIN HUBER ROSEN

Founder and Executive Director of Drink Local, Drink Tap

Erin Huber Rosen has a deep love of the Great Lakes—and not just the five in the U.S. As the founder and executive director of Drink Local, Drink Tap, she creatively connects local water conservation efforts to projects that provide safe water access to people in need across the globe.

Erin in her coworking space in Ohio City

The beginning

When I was little, I was very interested in being an astronaut. Then I wanted to start the women's NBA, which wasn't even a conversation yet, because I liked basketball. I also wanted to be the first female president.

I grew up on Lake Erie in Mentor, so many of my childhood memories were at Headlands Beach. We didn't have a lot of money, and going to the beach was something fun and free that our family always did. I felt very connected to water my whole life. When I started seeing pollution on the beach—plastic and other stuff—I wondered why it was there. As I got older, I started learning that we have so much more water right here than most people in the world. I began to learn about the world water crisis and got angry about the pollution I was seeing here because I knew people didn't have clean water, yet we were polluting what we had. I was about nine years old at the time.

My dad died when I was twelve. He always told me to speak up for things that can't stick up for themselves. He was my best friend, so going through my teenage years I really started to think about how I could make a difference in the world and take that lesson with me. Water connects a lot of equity and gender issues, so I knew if I worked in water, I could touch a lot of the things that I cared about.

Accidental nonprofit

Drink Local, Drink Tap started by accident. I don't typically tell people to start their own nonprofit. The world is already saturated with them. And it is very likely that someone else or some other organization can take your energy and pay you, and maybe you can do the fun stuff you envisioned to help solve the world's problems.

In 2009, I ended up in the water group of the Sustainable Cleveland Summit. Everybody was talking about all these big issues they cared about, like invasive species, combined sewer overflows, and lakefront access. After the summit, the group dwindled to about ten people. It was then that we decided to think about how the average person touches water every day. Most people can't connect to these big lake issues, but we thought maybe we could connect individual people to their individual use of water.

We were trying to get people to think about their disposable plastic bottle use, which kicked off a lot of energy around drinking tap water. We came up with the Drink Local, Drink Tap slogan, and it eventually became our name. As a group we wanted to do more, so we adopted Edgewater Park in 2010 and have cleaned up sixty-eight thousand pounds of trash since then. It's a great way to engage the general public in immediate, hands-on water issues. While we have those people by the lake, we're able to say, "Hey, did you know that we have 20 percent of the world's fresh surface water? Did you know that 2.5 billion people don't have access to safe water, taps, and toilets?" That's how we begin to make that local-to-global conversation happen.

Local to global

Back in 2010, I got asked by teachers and other educators to talk about the work we were doing. I went into schools to talk about local and global water issues and compare what those looked like. Both were passions of mine—I always wanted to work locally and globally, but I didn't know how that would happen. One day I was in an East Cleveland classroom talking about water to kids, and the teacher was from Uganda. She said her students were writing pen pal letters to kids in Uganda who were without water. And I thought, *That's it.* I went to East Africa to learn about what getting water is like there. I learned through my research as well as by making a documentary that 80 percent of water projects fail in the first two years. I saw a bunch of failed projects, learned why they failed and how to do it the right way, then set out to design, implement, and monitor water projects.

We have a 100 percent success rate for our projects, which comes from taking the time to develop relationships with people.

We have a 100 percent success rate for our projects, which comes from taking the time to develop relationships with people. I'm really proud that we get to know the communities that we partner with in Uganda. We make sure we're a good fit for each other. We have them contribute something toward the project so they have true ownership. We monitor the project long-term. International aid and development have been so savior-like, and they don't work. I think

if we all just stepped back for a minute and realized what our ego is driving versus what our heart is driving and what we actually have the capacity to do, there would be a lot less wasted money in the world.

We got our 501(c) nonprofit status in 2014. I really didn't feel the need to start a new nonprofit unless we had something unique and special. But at a certain point, our fiscal agent and some other mentors said we were ready to make that move. Even today, no one I know of in the U.S. is implementing, designing, and monitoring projects in a foreign country and doing such local grassroots action-based activities and education like we are. Anybody can do a beach cleanup. Anybody can go teach kids about water. It's the connection to global work that makes our nonprofit special.

Water is an equity issue

Even here in the U.S., the populations that are hit with water issues are living in poverty. Rural, Appalachian Americans, Native

Americans, people of color, and urban areas—those pockets of people tend to face more water issues. And I'm not talking about drought—I'm talking about access, connection, and polluted water sources.

In East Africa, the issues are a bit different. Though we work with poverty-stricken people, the water issues are everywhere—they're rampant. There are no clean freshwater sources anywhere except for deep in the ground. Little girls and women waste forty billion hours a year searching for water that is likely going to make their families sick. Water will kill a child under five every twenty seconds. It's an ongoing crisis that doesn't make the news. I also found out through my research that little girls who leave to go fetch water can get raped along the way and become early mothers. Guys hang out at the water sources and take advantage of these girls, who then drop out of school. Or, if girls don't have water to wash with at school, they just drop out. They don't have sanitary pads, so they have to take care of their periods in other ways.

I DON'T EXPECT EVERY PERSON TO TAKE THIS ON AS THEIR CAUSE. I JUST WANT EVERY PERSON TO CARE ABOUT SOMETHING OUTSIDE OF THEMSELVES.

Hustling, dreaming, burning out

The number of people who need clean water has actually increased since we started our work. So I constantly have to tell myself that what I'm doing is enough because you don't want to burn out and you can't take the burdens of the world on your shoulders. Your health will decline, you'll lose your friends and family, and you'll fall into depression. I caught myself in a few of those downfalls.

I've faced haters doing this work. Especially early on, some people didn't believe in me. Hearing some of those comments was very painful and sometimes immobilizing. I've lost friends along the way. For the first five years, this project involved twenty hours a day of hustling and dreaming and burning myself out and burning my friends out. There's also been a lot of competition—some of it nasty—in fundraising. Just because we are not a for-profit business doesn't mean we aren't in competition; we're in competition with a million other water organizations out there, and we have to make sure we invest in developing our brand.

I've started to study stoicism over the years, and that has really changed everything for me. Stoicism is really about recognizing that the only thing you can control in this life is your thoughts. If you learn how to guide those thoughts the right way, nothing else matters. No one else can make you think something. I'm a very deep, serious person, and this has helped me lighten up a little bit.

Learning and fulfillment every day

What I gained from this experience is fulfillment—every day. I get to use every minute of my life to do something that shifts the world. I've found true friends who have stayed with me through all the ups and downs. And I found my true partner in life, who wasn't just attracted to the shiny part of what I do. He's so supportive of the whole thing and has never asked me to change or shift my dream.

I'm proud of myself for sticking with it. I know there's a time to quit. Quitting is not bad—it's not failure. I truly believe that. Something deep inside just told me this was going to work. There were plenty of times when people told me to give up, or I told myself to. Or I was in holes of depression because I just couldn't see how this dream would ever really start functioning. I'm glad I stuck with it. It's involved learning every day and surrounding myself with people who can fill the gaps of what I can't do. I've been very lucky to have volunteers, board members, and mentors who have helped me grow.

If we want to help impact climate change in a positive way, we really need to rethink how we're developing not only the City of Cleveland but also the suburbs.

Our job as an organization is to open people's eyes. I used to get frustrated when people didn't care. But you can't make people care. There are also a lot of problems out there. I don't expect every person to take this on as their cause. I just want every person to care about something outside of themselves.

Why Cleveland?

I love the Great Lakes. No matter how much traveling I do, every time I come home there's a sense of relief. You can really be anybody and do anything here. There's space to be known and to create yourself.

An ideal picture of Cleveland

We would be a model for other Great Lakes cities of how to protect and speak up for our freshwater resources. In addition, we would be much more proactive in making sure that no one's water ever gets shut off and that everyone always has access to the water coming out of their taps and to their sewer.

I would love to see the City of Cleveland and Cuyahoga County do a lot more in regard to plastic pollution. It's extremely frustrating that the plastic bag ban can't get passed. The whole country of Rwanda went through genocide in the '90s, yet they don't allow plastic bags in their country. We have so much flexibility to make easy, sustainable changes, and we just haven't done it.

We also should have solved our lead paint issue a long time ago. We need to take that seriously because our kids are living with lifelong lead poisoning. It's the long-term unspoken Flint of Cleveland. We're killing our children with this lead paint issue. Regarding climate change, our urban tree canopy is suffering. If we want to help impact climate change in a positive way, we really need to rethink how we're developing not only the City of Cleveland but also the suburbs.

HEIDI CRESSMAN

Director of diversity and inclusion at
The University of Akron

Heidi Cressman is a tenacious engineer who specializes in the recruitment and retention of underrepresented groups into engineering programs at The University of Akron. She has developed a pipeline of outreach programs aimed at introducing engineering as a career option for K–12 students. She holds two patents.

Heidi at the
The University of Akron campus

The beginning

I was an intellectual type of kid. I had originally wanted to go to medical school because I thought I could help people. Then I talked to someone in med school who described how they cut open the human body, and that was all it took to dissuade me. That's when I decided I had to pick another field to go into. Since my dad was very happy as an engineer, I thought I might like it, too.

My parents didn't subscribe to gender roles, so I grew up playing with building toys and puzzles; they never gave Lincoln Logs just to my brother. Growing up, I didn't have a lot of challenges. My parents were very stable, I went to a suburban school, my friends were good people, and I grew up in a neighborhood that was, in my opinion, idyllic. I had luck.

While attending The University of Akron in the '80s, I was the only girl in some of my classes and didn't have anyone to connect with. I don't think I met another woman in engineering until my third year. Sometimes that was tough because I didn't feel as though I really fit in. It wasn't an awful experience—it's just that it was often lonely and isolating. I can see how, back then, this could have prevented some women from going through the program. As I got further along, I'd see fewer and fewer women in engineering classes because they would drop out eventually. When I finally did meet another woman on the engineering track, it changed my whole perspective because she was willing to lift me up. She wasn't competing with me—she was helping me get to a better place, and I appreciated that.

Trailblazing

One of the best things about engineering is getting to design something and actually see it work. It's rewarding to be able to make something better for someone else. I worked on a military project to develop a way to deploy a "black box"—which weighed about one thousand pounds—from a vehicle into the air using a telescoping mast. The purpose was to direct missiles to their target. Our goal was to put this communicative box up in the air and bring it back down in less than a minute in case the vehicle came under fire. I came up with a solution for it, was granted two patents, and was sent to Lockheed Martin for the installation into a Humvee. By being able to make the mechanical mast, we were supporting the military and helping to provide soldiers enough time to flee if they came under enemy fire.

As a mechanical engineer, I was the only woman in the engineering department. I was used to it, but it would have been nice to share the experience with another female. When I had my first baby, I had to walk from the company restroom through the engineering department to the kitchen to put my breast milk into the refrigerator. Even to ask for a chair in the bathroom took some courage. It was weird because none of my colleagues had to go to the restroom and pump when they had kids. All in all, the men I worked with were very supportive of me, and they thought it was great that a woman was working with them in the department. I admire the women who came before me because many of them didn't have any type of support.

> *It's crucial to move diversity forward in the engineering field because diverse thought leads to innovation.*

My work now stems from that experience. It's crucial to move diversity forward in the engineering field because diverse thought leads to innovation. Innovation is crucial to any company's success and for moving humanity forward in general. My role at The University of Akron has been to recruit and retain women and minority engineering students. We have programs for grades K–6, a summer camp for middle school students, Girl Scout events, and another set of events geared toward high school students. We encourage girls to return throughout their years so they eventually end up at The University of Akron. But, if they pursue STEM elsewhere, I still consider it a win.

As a university, most of our focus is on recruiting at the high school level, but I think encouraging diverse students should start much younger. A lot of students make up their minds in fourth grade about whether they're good at something. If they have the perception that they're not good at math, they're probably not going to pursue it. But if you give kids a growth mindset—which is the idea that nobody is born with math skills, and everybody has to learn them—they understand that you can always improve and learn to do anything.

Hope for the future

If I really believe in something, I'll figure out a way to make it happen. In a male-dominated field, there are good days and bad days. While working in the private sector, sometimes I would share an idea and it would get overlooked. Later, someone else would say the same thing, and everyone would think it was a great idea. When those things happened, I had to figure out when to speak up and when to just let it go. Although I did not always take credit for my ideas, it still felt good to see something come to fruition even without getting credit for it. Sometimes you just need to be glad if your idea is happening. There's a misconception that if women come into engineering roles, someone has to give something up, such as men losing jobs. But I don't think there has to be a loser in equality.

My current role in education isn't about the money—it's about passion. I really believe in the importance of diversity in engineering, and I believe in engineering as a phenomenal career choice, so I'm motivated to lead by example. What I've gained is hope for the future. In this position, I've had the chance to meet some of the brightest students I'll ever meet. I wouldn't trade it for anything. The best feeling is when I get a thank-you note from a young student who came to an event. Or, years later someone writes or calls me to say, "Hey, I made it." That means something—it shows that I can influence social norms and the results speak for themselves.

What is "success"?

Success to me means living in the moment. In any single moment, you can have success. It might be as simple as making it to work

I'VE HAD THE OPPORTUNITY TO DO A LOT OF FULFILLING THINGS. BUT I DIDN'T HAVE TO DO EVERYTHING AT THE SAME TIME AND BE A SUPERWOMAN.

on time that day. I've raised three daughters who are productive, kind, thoughtful, and open-minded—that's also a version of success.

One of my favorite quotes is, "Women can have it all, but they don't have to have it all at once." It rings true in my own life. I'm in a leadership position. I was a stay-at-home mom. I've had the opportunity to do a lot of fulfilling things. But I didn't have to do everything at the same time and be a superwoman.

I also think Sheryl Sandberg's analogy about a career path being like a jungle gym is pretty accurate because everyone's path in life and career is different. There are a lot of different ways to get where you want to go. She says getting to the top is never a straight ladder, and people rarely just rise to the top. Usually it's like climbing a jungle gym—you move a little sideways, then you move up, and you may have to go all the way around before you finally get a chance to reach the top.

An ideal picture of the Cleveland-Akron area

People bloom where they're planted and Northeast Ohio is a great place to bloom. I bristle when people talk negatively about Ohio. I think Ohio is one of the best states and I've been to all fifty of them! There is so much talent, creativity, and artistry in the region but it's the people that make it such a quality place to settle down.

An ideal version of the Cleveland-Akron area would be vibrant. This region would be a hotbed of technical knowledge, a place where gender roles become blurred, and barriers to education would be eliminated so that more women and minorities can discover the satisfaction of a career in STEM.

AC
KNOW
LEDGE
MENTS

Thank you to the twenty Boss Ladies who took time out of their busy schedules to be interviewed for this project. Getting to speak with you about your life's work was captivating and profound and best of all, fun. Thank you to the assistants who helped schedule and reschedule meetings, coordinated revisions, and showed excitement for this project. Thank you to Monica Farag, a Boss Lady in her own right, for designing these pages with as much style and poise as the women on them. Without you, this project would not be the same. Thank you to Ryan Gerard for being my trusty photo consultant and sounding board. Thanks to the early supporters and everyone who listened and said, "What a cool idea." Endless gratitude to you, the reader, for picking up this little book of stories—you were my biggest inspiration.

ABOUT

About the author

Maggie Sullivan is a writer, NPR nerd, classic ENFP, and dedicated dog mom from Cleveland. She earned a bachelor's degree in communication studies at Loyola University Chicago. *Boss Ladies of CLE* is her first book.

Website: bossladiescle.com
Instagram: @bossladiescle
Twitter: @bossladiescle
Facebook: @bossladiescle

About the designer

Monica Farag is a graphic designer and fashion blogger from Cleveland. She earned a bachelor's degree in visual communications design from Purdue University.

Website: doseofmonica.com
Instagram: @doseofmonica
Website: monicafarag.com
Instagram: @monicafaragdesign